Wagner Opera

11/6
$

AUDREY WILLIAMSON

Wagner Opera

Illustrated Calderbook CB.57

JOHN CALDER (PUBLISHERS) LTD. LONDON

THIS EDITION FIRST PUBLISHED IN GREAT BRITAIN 1962
BY JOHN CALDER (PUBLISHERS) LTD.
17 SACKVILLE STREET, LONDON, W.1
ALL RIGHTS RESERVED
© COPYRIGHT AUDREY WILLIAMSON 1962

MANUFACTURED BY MOUTON & CO. IN THE NETHERLANDS

782.1
W12Yw   Music

Wagner Opera

Contents

Wagner's birthplace at Leipzig

I Wagner's Life and Background

Richard Wagner was born at Leipzig on the 22nd of May, 1813:
but although he was christened under the name of his mother's
husband, there is considerable doubt that the Leipzig Police
Actuary, Carl Friedrich Wagner, was in fact his true father.
Carl Friedrich died six months after his birth, and in August, 1814,
his mother married the actor Ludwig Geyer, who had customarily
lived with the family during his annual seasons with the Leipzig
theatre company. Certainly their daughter, Richard's younger
sister Cäcilie, was born (in February, 1815) well before her legiti-
mate time, and towards the end of his life, after an apparent
revelation of Cäcilie's, Richard and his wife Cosima seem to have
accepted as practically certain the fact that Geyer was his father.

Inevitably he was brought up in an atmosphere steeped in the
theatre, and Carl Friedrich Wagner also had been an enthusiastic
playgoer and amateur actor, whose elder children naturally gravi-
tated to the stage. In the matter of heredity there is therefore little
to choose between the two candidates for paternity, beyond the
perhaps significant fact that Geyer's ancestry has been traced to
include a number of practising musicians, beginning with a Ben-
jamin Geyer who was town musician at Eisleben early in the
eighteenth century, and whose son and grandson were both or-
ganists (the latter, organist and cantor of St. Nicholas, Eisleben,
may well have studied the organ with Sebastian Bach, and certainly shared Wagner's combined passion for music and philosophy, for they were his chosen subjects of education at Leipzig).

7

It is interesting, too, that Geyer as an actor was hampered by his small height and weak voice in heroic parts – and lack of height and voice were probably the major factors in keeping Richard Wagner off the stage, although all who knew him in and out of the theatre testify to his supreme powers as an actor and teacher of actors when directing performances of his operas.

What is more to the point, as an influence in Wagner's background, was the fact that Geyer was enthusiastic in his application of the new Germanic style of 'naturalism' in acting – a reaction then in progress from Goethe's 'idealistic' method of projection. He was a reputedly good character actor interested in theory no less than practice, and a minor dramatist whose plays were performed in Dresden and a number of other provincial towns. He died when Richard was only six years old, but his influence was still pervasive in the struggling family of incipient actors, and home discussions doubtless fermented the intelligent boy's passionate interest in stage reform and dramatic interpretation.

This came to a head, with interesting creative results later, when in 1832, at the age of nineteen, he first heard the great dramatic singer Wilhelmine Schröder-Devrient (who at an early age had won over a truculent and suspicious Beethoven by her art) in a special performance of *Fidelio* at Leipzig. This "miracle", wrote Wagner in *Mein Leben*, "suddenly gave a new direction to my artistic feelings and exercised a decisive influence over my whole life... If I look back on my life as a whole, I can find no event that produced so profound an impression on me."

Schröder-Devrient – at that time, wrote Wagner, "at the zenith of her artistic career, young, beautiful and ardent, and whose like I have never again seen on the stage" – was to play an invaluable part in the presentation of Wagner's early operas and his developed ideal of performance; but in fact when he first saw her he had already settled on music, rather than the spoken drama, as his life's work. He had abandoned his plan of writing heroic tragedies in the manner of his idols, Shakespeare and the Greek dramatists, when at the age of fourteen he attended one of the famous Leipzig Gewandhaus concerts and heard Beethoven's Seventh Symphony for the first time. The effect on him was, in his own words, 'indescribable''. Since the German opera houses of that day combined a repertoire of plays and opera, and often expected its actors to appear in both (Geyer had sung minor tenor rôles for Weber, the music director at Dresden), he could not have been totally unaware

8

of music until that time; but his background and education were
wholly dramatic, and the concert on the 17th of January, 1828, lit a
spark in him of which up to that moment he had certainly been
unaware.

Wilhelmine Schröder-Devrient (the original Senta and Venus)

It was indeed late to start, from the professional point of view,
and it was many years before Wagner attained the mastery and ease
of technique which came in little more than childhood to Mozart
and other major composers. That Wagner was a born musician his
rapid progress and the genius of his scores (a genius the processes
of which he never had to analyse like those of his painstakingly-

written librettos) indicate; but only a nature, in addition, of his immense energy and artistic conscientiousness could have conquered so completely an art with little external tuition, and the inevitable sense in the early years that he was battling against lost time.

Wagner, however, had no qualms and certainly no hesitations. From the lending library of Friedrich Wieck (father of Clara Schumann) he immediately borrowed Logier's *Method of General-bass*, and began his secret study of musical composition at the expense of the family purse and temper (when his activities were discovered) and his formal education. Partly through circumstance, partly by nature, he was a self-educator in music: the lessons in harmony he took from the violinist of the theatre orchestra, Christian Müller, were not wholly successful, and he learnt most through plunging direct into the scores of the great composers, which he soon read fluently.

The creative instinct within him was already so strong that he had no sooner mastered the viola clef in order to study a quartet by Haydn, than he composed a string quartet of his own! Orchestration he studied from the full score of *Don Giovanni* and at seventeen, within two years of his discovery of his musical bent, he copied the full score of Beethoven's Ninth Symphony and made an arrangement of it for piano solo. This so impressed Schotts, the publishers, that the following year they sent him a full score of the Mass in D. This was the foundation of a knowledge and understanding of Beethoven – including the last quartets – few possessed at the time, and Wagner as a conductor and music director later was to take a principal part in spreading this appreciation, especially in connection with the Choral Symphony, till then considered almost unperformable.

His method of learning by copying scores was eminently sound; his vital individualism absorbed all he needed to know without in any way losing its personal imprint. The major resources were within him, untouched by too-rigid Beckmesser rules and free therefore to mature along lines of innovation and instinctive fecundity. But the dramatic background was too pressing to be shelved from his artistic outlook: it was absorbed into and transformed by the new passion for music, and the ideal of a new style of opera and interpretation, the music-drama in which all arts of the theatre – singing, orchestral score, design, drama and acting – coalesced, began early to form in Wagner's urgent and restless mind.

10

Many years later, Fokine and Diaghileff were to come to a similar diagnosis of theatrical-musical collaboration and create a comparable revolution in their particular sphere of ballet.

Meanwhile, Wagner inevitably was more bound to his immediate musical precedents. Weber, who had been created director of the Dresden Opera House in 1817, was a principal influence, as he was throughout the German states. In 1821 his *Der Freischütz* was produced in Berlin and the following year in Dresden, and Wagner was early impressed by it and shared something of the general enthusiasm. Certainly his first operas owe more than a little to *Der Freischütz*: in their Faustian themes, and in the supernatural forces at work in the atmosphere of *The Flying Dutchman*, no less than its Spinning Chorus which has a prototype in Act III, Scene 1 of Weber's opera. Even Weber's use of *parlando* (notably in a scene between Kaspar and Max) was a dim herald of Wagner's own development of a new form of recitative to bind the music together.

Lohengrin owed even more to Weber's *Euryanthe*. Only after this work, the last of his operas still tied partly to convention and the four-square rhythm, did he break from the old traditions and, after a long rest from composition, produce the revolutionary music-dramas which opened up a new epoch symphonically no less than operatically. Here he left behind the theatre format of strings with woodwind and brass in pairs, and in *The Ring* demanded woodwind and brass in larger groups, adding the English horn, bass clarinet, double bassoon and bass trumpet – augmented by special tubas, percussion and harps as required. The result was a richer and more powerful texture of scoring than any opera house had ever known; yet used not just for power but with a luminous variety of orchestration and *nuances* of sound which gave to his stage dramas unusual musical subtlety and delicacy, no less than force and passion.

The revolution was so complete that Wagner himself realised it would imply a new style of training for singers and a new type of theatre in which the blend of voice and instruments could only be perfectly balanced by the placing of the orchestra out of sight under the stage. That he achieved even this, at the end of a long and exhausting struggle against penury, debt and musical calumny, was a result of the heroic courage and integrity of the composer and, one is forced by his story to believe, a destiny which in the end must always give way to genius.

11

Little of this could have been envisaged when Wagner's first Piano Sonata in B Flat Major was published in 1832 – dedicated to Theodor Weinlig, the greatest living contrapuntist with whom alone Wagner studied with real benefit. The same year saw two overtures performed at concerts in Leipzig and Dresden, and the following January his Symphony in C Major made an appearance at a Gewandhaus concert. In 1833, at the age of twenty, Wagner obtained his first position as solo and chorus rehearser at the Würzburg Theatre, where his brother Albert was tenor and stage manager, and worked on his first opera, *Die Feen*, which was not performed until 1888 at Munich, five years after his death. Disappointments over this opera did not prevent his starting another, *Das Liebesverbot*, the plot of which derived from Shakespeare's *Measure for Measure*, but which Wagner transplanted to a Sicilian setting. It was finished in the New Year of 1836 and rehearsed at Magdeburg in March, without ever, owing to theatre upheavals and public indifference, reaching the stage (Wagner, presenting the score to King Ludwig of Bavaria in 1866, referred to it as the "sin of my youth").

Wagner's engagement as music director at Magdeburg in 1834 was momentous in another way: he fell violently in love with a pretty actress at the theatre, Minna Planer, and married her on the 24th of November, 1836. Domestically a marriage which both fought long to preserve, and with some compensations for the overworked and hardpressed Wagner, it was intellectually incompatible and dis-

12

Wagner's first wife, Minna Planer

astrous, and only the hard concrete of Wagner's essential egoism
and artistic integrity probably saved him from bowing to easy
success, in the face of mounting debt and Minna's total inability
to understand why he could no longer meet the public demand
for operas in his early 'popular' style.

In the Autumn of 1837 the Wagners moved on to Riga, where
he remained as Kapellmeister at the theatre for two years, pro-
ducing and conducting a repertory of fifteen operas during the
first year and twenty-four the second. This taxing volume of work
did not prevent his launching into the composition of his third
opera, *Rienzi*. Already he knew composition to be his major interest
and, weighed down by the extraneous demands of his work at the
theatre, his growing burden of debt and the "domestic tribulations",
as he later described them, already attendant on his marriage, he
found his only peace of mind in this escape into historical fiction.
The work showed a new seriousness and brilliance of musical
invention (according to the standards of the time), and, produced at
Dresden in 1842, was to prove for many years – long, in fact, after
he had musically far outgrown it – his greatest theatrical success.

Only the lack of any copyright safeguards in that period, indeed,
prevented Wagner achieving any financial stability in his early and
middle years as a composer. For the greater part of his life he
suffered from the procedure by which German state theatres se-
cured the rights of limitless performance of a work after one small
original payment, and Wagner was in the ironic position of being
without money often to continue composition while his early
operas were constantly produced, with public success, throughout
Germany. It explains and excuses much in respect of his notorious
financial difficulties and reputation as a hopeless borrower; and it
is not entirely surprising that his character in this respect hardened
and degenerated with time. In later years his passion for luxury,
which he seems to have found congenitally necessary to ease the
strains of ill-health and overwork, certainly outweighed his sense of
honour as a debtor; but the appalling burdens of his early life as a
musician never induced him to deviate from his highest artistic
aims, and the shame must rest on the public treatment of the artist
in society at least as much as on the often desperate measures forced on him for survival.

It was his dangerous position regarding his creditors that obliged
him to leave Riga in 1839. With his wife and the encumbrance of a
huge St. Bernard dog, Robber (throughout his life Wagner was

never without a dearly beloved and devoted canine 'retainer'), he set sail on a small merchant vessel, the *Thetis*, in a plan to reach Paris (Mecca of the opera composer's dreams) *via* London. It was a turbulent and historical journey which was to provide much inspiration for the tempestuous seascapes of his next opera, *The Flying Dutchman*. Safely if shakenly ashore, the travellers survived what Wagner, no puritan, described with feeling as "the horrors of a ghastly London Sunday", as well as Robber's alarming adventurous bent for lone exploration of the foreign city, and eleven days later, on the 20th of August, they proceeded to Paris.

The 'Mecca', of course, failed entirely to rise to its Wagnerian responsibilities. It was the age of Meyerbeer and frivolous operatic tastes, and although Wagner made some abortive musical contacts the period of three years in Paris was one of the most bitter and frustrating of his life. *Rienzi* found no willing producer, he was forced in sheer poverty to live almost wholly by sporadic journalism, and the only influence of value was perhaps his introduction to the music of Berlioz – himself struggling to get his vast and original works before the public. He also met Liszt here for the first time: but Liszt's lifelong friendship with and loyal artistic admiration of the younger man, of major importance in Wagner's life and career, were not firmly established until later. In the meantime, the frightening gap between opulence and poverty in the Paris world formed political roots in Wagner which came to disastrous flower in the Dresden Revolution of 1849.

In Paris, Wagner, nevertheless, completed the scoring of *Rienzi* and began work on *The Flying Dutchman*. In November, 1840, he sent the *Rienzi* score to the Dresden theatre, mainly because the principal tenor there, Tichatschek, seemed to him the only singer in Germany likely to meet the vocal requirements of the heroic leading part, and because Schröder-Devrient also was on the strength of the opera house. It was accepted in June, 1841, and produced the following year, Wagner leaving Paris to supervise the production and take up the post of principal conductor at the opera house. In spite of its unwieldy length and perhaps because of its spectacular scenic demands (over which Wagner, the stage reformer and perfectionist, went through his normal agonies of apprehension), the opera was a dazzling success. Tichatschek, most unusually lovable and good-natured of tenors, became Wagner's faithful slave for life in gratitude for his heroic part and gorgeous silver armour. For many years, in spite of some defects

14

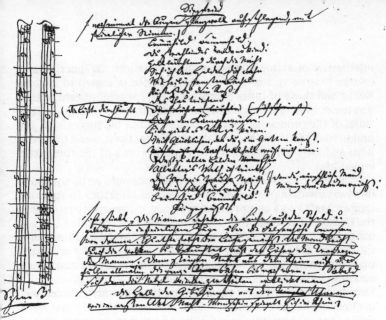

Faksimile aus der Originalhandschrift des ersten Entwurfs zu Siegfried's Tod, vom Jahre 1848.
Beilage zu Chamberlain, Richard Wagner.

Facsimile of the first draft of 'Siegfrieds Tod', 1848

by Wagner's demanding standards, he was indispensable in Wagnerian rôles, the only *heldentenor* to do the operas vocal and dramatic justice until the time when Wagner could take a personal hand in the training of his singers.

The next year, 1843, *The Flying Dutchman* was produced at Dresden, following an unsuccessful attempt to get this stormy vessel launched in Berlin, and on the 19th of October, 1845, *Tannhäuser* followed. Already Wagner, too, had been attracted by the anonymous epic of *Lohengrin* and worked out a sketch for the opera. Yet during this creative stimulus and development of ideas (which included the first sketch for *Die Meistersinger*, like all Wagner's works long in gestation and the greater in genius for it), he carried out the exhaustive duties of Royal Kapellmeister and conductor – the last an art in which he showed a flexibility and sensitivity of phrasing almost unknown in his age, and of great eventual influence on conducting generally. By modern standards, there is no doubt orchestras and singers of the period had serious defects, and

15

intelligence of acting and presentation was low. Wagner's was a constant battle against such conditions both in regard to his own works and those of other composers, and his achievement in time was invaluable. But it is hardly surprising that the thought, in later exile, of the production of his operas without his supervision and undoubtedly far from his own dramatic intentions, was a torture to him, and only his turning to the mature works of the future sustained him.

In 1849 the crash came. Wagner's politics were certainly bound up always with his experiences and needs as an artist. In spite of a long struggle and a comprehensive Report on necessary reforms to the Dresden Theatre authorities, which was rejected in 1847, he had made small headway in his fight for artistic standards (including the raising of the appallingly low salaries to attract better orchestral players) against the immovable weight of bureaucracy and Court, and for a time – especially after the rejection of *Lohengrin* by Dresden in 1848 – it must have seemed that the only panacea was, in effect, a change of political state. His pamphlet, *Art and Revolution*, one of a multitudinous body of writings on music, drama, metaphysics and philosophy published during his lifetime (and themselves almost a life's work for a professional writer), canalised his discontent, and it is certain he was more or less deeply involved in the outbreak of revolution in Dresden in 1849. Roeckel and Bakoonin, chief among his socialist friends, were imprisoned and Wagner, with a writ on his head, was forced to flee to Switzerland.

There, in Zurich, he remained for ten years of exile, taking some active part in the musical life in the town, and in the first comparative peace of his life bringing to creation *Das Rheingold* and *Die Walküre* of the *Ring* cycle (the poems, *Siegfrieds Tod* first, had been sketched in the Dresden period) and the revolutionary *Tristan und Isolde*. (It is amusing that Wagner set aside *Siegfried* to embark on this with the idea of providing his publishers with a 'popular' opera to offset financially his more 'difficult' works! The mature musician was now too deeply developed in him to produce anything but a complex and progressive orchestral score.) It was, in fact, twelve years before he took up *Siegfried* again. He had left his hero, he wrote to Liszt wistfully in 1857, "under a linden tree" (in the second act in the forest), and "said farewell to him". But it was *Tristan*, the intruder on the Nibelungen saga, that Wagner always referred to later as his "child of sorrow".

Although the idea had occurred to him a few years previously,

16

the opera was composed in 1857 under the pressure of an idealistic romance with the beautiful young wife of a rich industrialist, Otto Wesendonck, who was most generous to Wagner. There is no doubt Mathilde Wesendonck was much in Wagner's thoughts during the creation of both Sieglinde and Isolde; the flame, in fact that was already lighting up the rapturous Spring song, *Du Bist der Lenz*, of Sieglinde, flared into the veritable conflagration of the more passionate character of Isolde. As always with Wagner – whose love affairs, on close analysis, prove to be infinitely fewer and more sublimated than popular scandal would suggest – the creative inspiration fastened itself on a temporarily charming and congenial person, rather than the other way about. The Wesendonck affair was brief and almost certainly blameless (in fact, though the friendship waned; Wagner met the couple on amiable terms several times in later life); but it involved a domestic torment with Minna – now distorted in nerves and mind through an incurable heart disease and deeply resentful of the serious change of direction of Wagner's musical style – and this finally broke up the idyll of their peaceful retreat, the small house 'Asyl', on the Wesendonck estate.

To Mathilde, however, we also owe the group of five 'Wesen-

Richard Wagner
*ehemal. Kapellmeister und politischer Flüchtling
aus Dresden.*

Die Nr. 140 der „Leipziger Zeitung" vom 20. Mai 1849 brachte folgenden Original-

Steckbrief.

Der unten etwas näher bezeichnete Königl. Capellmeister

Richard Wagner von hier
ist wegen wesentlicher Theilnahme an der in hiesiger Stadt stattgefundenen aufrührerischen Bewegung zur Untersuchung zu ziehen, zur Zeit aber nicht zu erlangen gewesen. Es werden daher alle Polizeibehörden auf denselben aufmerksam gemacht und ersucht, Wagnern im Betretungsfalle zu verhaften und davon uns schleunigst Nachricht zu ertheilen.

Dresden, den 16. Mai 1849.

Die Stadt-Polizei-Deputation.

von Oppell.

Wagner ist 37—38 Jahre alt, mittler Statur, hat braunes Haar und trägt eine

Facsimile of the warrant for Wagner's arrest after the Dresden Revolution, 1849

donck' songs Wagner composed at this time to poems she had written, two of them using themes later developed in the opera; and the miraculously pervasive poignancy of the *Tristan* score, a monument indeed to human sorrow and ill-starred ecstasy and devotion, will always be associated to some extent with her. Further influences were Wagner's new interests in Schopenhauer (whom he met at Zurich) and Buddhism, although his study of the latter, like the Wesendonck affair, seems rather to have grown out of the creative idea than the contrary.

Wagner's reputation at last was growing, not a little due to Liszt's productions of *Tannhäuser* and *Lohengrin* in 1849 and 1850 at Weimar, where he now held the principal Court musical position.* These set alight a demand for Wagner's operas throughout Germany and abroad. Some Wagner Festival concerts at Zurich in May, 1853, also greatly raised his prestige; and the same year saw the first production of a Wagner opera – *Tannhäuser* – at his birthplace, Leipzig. In 1855 he had also conducted a series of Philharmonic concerts in London, Queen Victoria and Prince Albert attending the seventh concert, when the *Tannhäuser* overture was repeated "by command". The press as always was mainly antagonistic: but by now Wagner had built up a loyal band of devoted followers and with the public his success was never very seriously in doubt.

The full score of Act II of *Tristan* was finished on the 9th of March, 1859, at Venice, where Wagner had fled following the Wesendonck crisis (Minna having opened a letter of his to Mathilde – the contents of which, it was proved when it was published many years later, she had greatly distorted and exaggerated – he had left the two women to fight out the issue between them; which they did, in his absence, without much quarter on either side). By the 9th of August the entire work was completed at Lucerne. In 1860 he was again in Paris, where he met Rossini – "the only really great musician", he wrote, whom he had met there – and made a favourable impression on him. The failure of his *Tannhäuser* at the Paris Opéra in March, 1861, after great trouble and long rehearsals on Wagner's part, was a disgraceful episode due entirely to the influential social *claque* known as the Jockey Club, young men about town who resented the placing of the ballet in the first act (forcing them into the unusual necessity of turning up for the

* It was not until 1861, in Vienna, that Wagner himself was able to see a stage performance of *Lohengrin*.

Mathilde Wesendonck

Wagner in middle life

beginning of the opera) and interrupted the three performances with whistles and riots, which the resentment of the rest of the audience could not quell. But we owe to this production, nevertheless, Wagner's revised and maturer scoring of the Venusberg music generally, and although he resented the necessity to meet Parisian taste with a ballet at all, he made the best of a bad job in his score.

Wagner's true hopes had been pinned on gaining custody of his Paris royalties on *Rienzi* and a Paris production of *Tristan*: both were disappointed. But in 1860, after long and fruitless negotiation, his official exile from Germany came to an end, and in January, 1862, he completed the poem of *Die Meistersinger* in high hopes, although in fact the opera was not finally scored until 1867, and produced until 1868 (at Munich). It is a measure of his international reputation, in spite of vicious critical attack and his own dejected feeling that his true musical-dramatic aims were not fully understood even by his admirers, that in 1862 he was invited to conduct in St. Petersburg, where his third programme included excerpts from *The Ring*, and where his triumph both artistically and in Court circles was unchallengeable.

The real turning point of his life, however, came in 1864. By an amazing stroke of luck of the kind Fate sometimes holds up its sleeve for the flabbergasted recipient, the new youthful King of Bavaria, Ludwig II, who succeeded his uncle on the throne in March of that year, had since a boy of twelve been an infatuated devotee of Wagner's music and had already by royal command achieved productions of *Lohengrin* and *Tannhäuser* in his capital, Munich. An avid reader, too, of Wagner's reformatory theories in *Opera and Drama* and other works, and an isolated romantic idealist by nature, the young King, now eighteen years old, marked the opening of his reign with a determination to share in Wagner's great work by freeing him financially to continue creation.

Few of the more grandiose plans – including a new Opera House for Wagner's works at Munich – came to fruition, and Wagner's stay in Munich was cut short by scandal and political resentment some months after the first performance of *Tristan* the following year. But the King's stipend remained to the end of his life and his admiration, and at least a large part of his personal devotion to Wagner, survived the Cosima scandal and the shifting of Wagner's interest to the new theatre constructed for his works at Bayreuth.

21

Ludwig II, King of Bavaria

It is characteristic of public and political distrust of the arts that Ludwig's passion for them should have given him eventually a reputation for 'madness'. As a King he was a misfit who nevertheless tried conscientiously for a time (and urged, it must be admitted, by Wagner) to carry out his state obligations, not without shrewdness and intelligence. When he lost Wagner, partly owing to the jealousy of his politicians, he turned in time to costly and fabulous architectural schemes, which drained the public exchequer far more than music had done. An unhappy, lonely young man, a remorseful secret homosexual with conflicting ideals of chastity and artistic purity, he was liquidated (as our hardly more civilised age would put it) by his politicians by means of a declaration of his insanity (signed by four doctors who had not even examined him) in 1886, three years after Wagner's death. Being far too sane not to realise what his future life would be, he committed suicide in the lake of his lodge at Starnberg, and thus avoided the final loss of his freedom.

His monuments are *The Ring* and *Parsifal*, which might never have been completed without his help, and the first production of *Tristan* which itself was marked by tragedy: the death of the Tristan, the young Ludwig Schnorr von Carolsfeld – an artist in whom Wagner at last found the actor and singer of his dreams – on the 21st of July, 1865, only three weeks after the third *Tristan* performance at Munich on the 28th of June. It was the greatest blow in Wagner's life as a producer: three years later he commememorated his unshaken sorrow and admiration in a book on the dead singer, and he mourned the first and greatest of his Tristans to the end of his days.

Wagner's extravagance made him unpopular in Munich, but the

Ludwig Schnorr von Carolsfeld as Lohengrin

real cause of his exile, though it did not become fully apparent till later, was his liaison with Liszt's daughter, Cosima von Bülow, whose young husband, Hans, was a Wagnerian devotee and the conductor in whom Wagner placed most trust. It had not been a happy marriage for Cosima, brought about mainly, it would seem, from Bülow's respect for Liszt; and although Bülow had an undoubted and profound admiration for Cosima's qualities, which had been a great staple to his highly strung nature, he seems temperamentally never to have been really attuned to matrimony. Nevertheless, and although it is apparent now that he had been an acquiescent member of the 'triangle' up to a point, his sufferings in the face of open scandal were considerable, and it was some years before he could be induced to divorce Cosima.

Minna died in 1866, having long lived apart from Wagner, who made her a generous allowance; but from 1865 until 1870 Wagner and Cosima were forced to face out or veil the situation as best they could at 'Triebschen', near Lucerne, a beautiful house where Wagner could work in idyllic surroundings and where his three children by Cosima – Isolde, Eva and at last the longed-for son Siegfried – made a happy home for him with the two elder von Bülow children, Daniela and Blandine. It was on Christmas Day, 1870, that Wagner celebrated Cosima's thirty-third birthday and the birth of his son with the now-famous per-

Wagner at 'Triebschen', 1868

formance of the *Siegfried Idyll*, played by a few local instrumentalists on the stairs outside her room.

After long travail this was to prove for him the ideal union. His sunset brightened in the warmth of Cosima's early summer, and there is no doubt, although to others she had some irritating qualities (an ingrained anti-semitism, fanning Wagner's own, born perhaps of financial envy, was among them), she was to him a partner completely in tune intellectually: able to stimulate the work of his last years and stabilise it at Bayreuth after his death. They were married in 1870, by which time the plans to produce *The Ring* at a newly-built theatre in Bayreuth were well under way: but although they moved there in 1871 and took up residence in their house, 'Wahnfried', it was not until 1876 that the completed saga and theatre could, in fact, come together in a first, ideal (or as near ideal as Wagner could make it) performance.

Here at last, clouded only by the conscientiously miserable Bayreuth climate, years of planned reform in the presentation of a new style of music-drama ended in triumph. An artistic triumph, at least, for Wagner had chosen his singers carefully from the best

24

Festival Theatre, Bayreuth

Villa Wahnfried: Wagner's house at Bayreuth

of the German opera houses, subjected them to long rehearsal with
a year's study of their parts and the score behind them, personally
supervised the production in every detail, trained the orchestra,
and placed it in the position he had long advocated to enable his
orchestral genius to flower without overwhelming the vocal line –
out of sight under the stage. That in spite of full houses, and an
audience rich in international musicians, it failed financially was,
in view of the outlay (Ludwig had once again come to the rescue
with a state loan), not entirely surprising; although the blow to
Wagner of not being able to repeat the Festival annually was heavy.
It was not, in fact, until 1882 that the Festspielhaus again opened
its doors to the public, when sixteen performances of *Parsifal*,
Wagner's last work, were given between the 26th of July and the
29th of August. Again there was the most careful and prolonged
rehearsal, this time with duplicate casts. The orchestra numbered
107, and owing apparently to a sudden indisposition of Hermann
Levi, the conductor, Wagner himself conducted the last performance on the 29th of August from the Transformation music
onwards.

It was his final contact with the theatre, and he knew it would be
his last work, For some time his heart had been giving rise to

With Cosima, 1883: the last photograph

Venice: Palazzo Vendramin Calergi where Wagner died

anxiety, and the truth is the stupendous struggle and achievement had at last worn out the scarred old warrior, now in his seventieth year – although his colossal energy and youthfulness had long concealed some of the strain beneath. Nevertheless, the financial success (8,200 tickets were sold and realised 240,000 marks) stimulated Wagner to new plans for the 1883 Festival. With some of the old magic still shimmering (he could be a gay, beguiling companion and talker in spite of his inflammable temper and occasional virulence), he set off out of the grey Bayreuth climate to Venice on the 14the of September, arriving there on the 16th. He never left. On the late afternoon of the 13th of February, 1883, he died suddenly, in Cosima's arms, following a heart attack. For twenty-five hours she refused to leave his side and could not be induced to eat. "*Soeur, il faut vivre*", telegraphed the forgiving Bülow, hearing of her plight. Then the funeral cortège set out on its long wintry journey to Bayreuth, where Wagner was buried.

It was forty-seven years before Cosima joined him in death. But by then, partly owing to her unremitting efforts, Bayreuth and Wagner were accepted legends of the musical world.

Wagner's grave at Bayreuth

'The Flying Dutchman': Hermann Uhde as the Dutchman

II The Flying Dutchman

Although *The Flying Dutchman* was the second of Wagner's operas to obtain any hold in the German opera repertoire, it is the first of his works to have survived outside Germany, and the first to show anything of his later direction as a composer of music-drama. "It was", wrote Wagner, "the first folk-poem that forced its way into my heart, and called on me as a man and an artist to point its meaning and mould it as a work of art." It is by far the shortest of his works,* and was in fact originally planned as a one-act opera: perhaps as a rebound from the production difficulties created by *Rienzi*, the first and second acts alone of which at its first performance, lasted as long as Weber's *Der Freischütz*, and the excessive length of which, even after cutting, has always been found to be unmanageable since its original popularity in Germany waned.

Wagner based his own *Flying Dutchman* scenario largely on Heine's version, although the legend of the Dutchman forced to sail the seas for ever, after an oath overheard by the Devil that he would round the Cape at Table Bay in tempestuous seas or be eternally damned, dated back to the sixteenth century and had an earlier parallel also, of course, in the story of the Wandering Jew – used by Wagner in the Kundry character in his last opera, *Parsifal*. Sir Walter Scott and Captain Marryat (in *The Phantom Ship*) are other writers who have dealt with the legend, and there was also a

* Excepting, of course, *Das Rheingold*, the prelude of the *Ring* cycle.

31

play by Fitzball in London in 1825, as well as another, by W. G. Wills and Percy Fitzgerald, in 1878 at the Lyceum Theatre, with no less an actor than Sir Henry Irving in the rôle of the Dutchman, Vanderdecken.

This may have been partly inspired by the first English production of Wagner's *The Flying Dutchman* at Drury Lane in 1870: in fact, the very first performance of a Wagner opera in England – twenty-seven years after its original production in Dresden, and in Italian (under the title *L'Olandese Dannato*) at that! Sir Charles Santley sang the part of Vanderdecken. At about the same time Wagner, now in the full maturity of his powers, revised *The Flying Dutchman* overture, lightening the orchestration in particular with regard to the brass. He also in his late years considered remoulding the opera into one act form, but never lived to do this.

The overture now seems the most descriptive and original concentration of music in the opera, although it is rare for this to be revealed in performance by a conductor who is artist enough to avoid bombast and observe Wagner's own much more varied and sensitive markings in the score. It is easy to see from it, and some of the later use of the orchestra and of the *motifs* in the overture, how marked its individuality must have seemed to the public of the time; but by the standard of Wagner's later works the opera as a whole is now curiously old-fashioned, with a highly Italianate arrangement of *arias*, duets and *ensembles*, the tunes of some of which are conventional to their period and hardly in the same class as the middle (let alone later) Verdi. Nor is the 'book' entirely happy, though earlier English critics, who despised the music, were surprisingly enthusiastic about it. Wagner took from Heine the idea of the woman whose unchanging love can alone release the Dutchman from his curse, but his characterisation is thin and his plot at moments 'stagey' and wholly artificial. What he did achieve was a certain musical-dramatic power in the atmosphere of the sea and the supernatural, something original to himself and still wholly recognisable when compared with his mature works.

In his poverty-stricken period in Paris in 1841 he had been forced, with great bitterness, to part with the French rights of his story (in 'sketch' form) for 500 francs: the Paris Opéra only being willing to produce it if it were set by another composer, Pierre Dietsch. Dietsch's *Le Vaisseau Fantôme* was produced at the Opéra on the 9th of November, 1842, and was soon as phantasmal as the vessel.

It is interesting to note that this forgotten composer in 1861 conducted the Paris version of *Tannhäuser* at the Opéra, and there is no doubt that in comparison with his *Vaisseau Fantôme* Wagner's own opera had at least the vitality of genius. It is, indeed, on that vitality and its stage effect that it has sustained its popularity in the theatre to this day.

The sea- and wind-saturated overture opens with a shivering figure on strings and woodwind: at the end of the second bar the principal theme of the whole opera appears on horns and bassoons in the bass – the *motif* of the curse-ridden Dutchman:

Four bars later it reappears on trombones and tuba, and on other instruments continues to be heard among the descriptive musical evocation of singing winds and lashing seas until a pizzicato echo on cello and double bass, and three beats on the kettledrum, signify the momentary dying down of the storm and allow the soft theme of Senta's ballad (the theme of her 'self-sacrifice') to be heard for the first time:

This immediately rises an octave on oboe, clarinet and horns, with flutes sounding in the final three notes; and indeed Wagner's use of woodwind and horns in this overture anticipates his later work and often has a delicacy that serenely relieves the energy and agitation of the atmosphere. Later we hear the Dutchman's opening solo in the first act, and the sailors' chorus from the last; and after elaborate development, still full of the sea-swept atmosphere, Senta's ballad and the Curse return to dominate the end. Although there is no leading *motif* development in this opera in at all the same sense, orchestrally, as in *The Ring*, these first and last two overture themes are to return at dramatically appropriate moments many times in the score.

The first act now begins with no diminution of the musical seascape: we are on the shore of the rocky Norwegian bay of Sandwike (the same, it is said, as that in which Wagner's vessel took refuge during his three-week storm-tossed journey from Riga to London). The tempest still rages, and the Norwegian Captain, Daland, has cast anchor in the hope of temporary shelter. On his ship the crew are noisily active and Daland himself is standing on a rock. (Wagner can surely be acquitted of real ignorance of navigation, strange though it may seem at times in this opera, with ships anchored on the shore and characters easily leaping from them to dry land. It was, after all, a necessary dramatic licence, while preserving the sea effects on the stage.)

The sailors are singing a chorus of a 'Yo-ho' nature, echoed on the horns, and Daland is regretting that though he had actually seen his house from the sea, his ship had been blown seven miles away from it, and his daughter Senta, by the storm. He returns to deck and leaves the Steersman to keep watch, while the storm abates and returns at intervals. The Steersman is sleepy and his song, comparable in some ways to the sailor's opening song in *Tristan**, is preceded by a figure of two notes on the horn which are to reappear in the score:

Eventually he falls asleep, the violence of the storm increases, and in the darkness we now see the luminous approaching ship of the Flying Dutchman, with blood-red sails and black mast (Curse theme on horns and bassoons). At the crash of its anchor the Steersman starts up, but humming a fragment of his tune falls asleep again. And while his spectral crew furl the sails, the Dutchman himself, a pale, morose figure in black, steps ashore.

He has come on land at the end of a seven-year phase at sea; for he is allowed this periodic release to search for the woman who alone, by her love, will release him from his curse. His recitative and *aria, Wie oft in Meerestiefsten Schlund*, describe this doom in a sombre bass-baritone, underlined by the surging sea and the Curse *motif*; and he darkly remembers how often, in anguish, he had

* Could Wagner have been inspired by a similar sailor's song (also for tenor) on Aeneas' departing ship in Berlioz' *The Trojans?* As *The Flying Dutchman* was composed so close to his Paris period, it seems not unlikely.

34

dashed his ship against the rocks in a vain attempt to end his life. Apart from this anguish, and longing for release, the Dutchman is not psychologically at all developed by Wagner: but his stage presence can be theatrically effective – pallid-faced, gloomy and ghostly, a figure apart.

His final despairing cry, mirroring his endless doom:

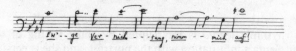

Ew---ge Ver-nich---tung, nimm---mich auf!

is mysteriously echoed by his ship's crew, and we hear the Curse again before Daland comes out of his cabin and sees the strange ship. He angrily wakes the Steersman, who calls to the newcomer's crew without effect: then Daland notices the Dutchman and exchanges storm-comments with him. The stranger admits only his race and gloomily recounts his long wanderings on the sea, and then abruptly asks the Norwegian if he could shelter for a night in his home. He offers much treasure on his ship as a bribe, and with even more startling abruptness asks Daland if he has a daughter. On Daland's affirmative, he immediately requests her hand in marriage (it is one of several moments in which Wagner strains our credulity to the limit). Daland's cupidity is aroused, and during a duet of longing on one side, and curiosity on the other, the unspeakable (and unbelievable) father gladly agrees to the match. He then suggests, as the storm has abated, both ships shall sail for his home.

All this has been in the most conventional Italian operatic style, with a little dancing tune accompanying Daland's suggestion. But the sailors' chorus (on the Steersman's theme of the maiden to whom each longs to return) brings a fresher sea element, and the act ends with a reiteration of the two-note figure that preceded the Steersman's song.

We hear it again in the Introduction to the second act, which opens gaily in Daland's house, where a bevy of young girls, led by Senta's nurse Mary, are spinning. A picture of the legendary Dutchman is prominent on the wall, and to this the eyes of Senta, sitting idle in a chair, frequently turn. She is a young girl with a quality of mystic vision we are to find again in Elsa in *Lohengrin*; remote from the others, and certainly not (ideally) the solid soprano of stage tradition.

35

The famous Spinning Chorus is as tuneful as something out of Gilbert and Sullivan (one thinks, in fact, especially of the chorus of *contadine* in *The Gondoliers*), although its inspiration was doubtless, as already mentioned, a similar song in *Der Freischütz:*

The rhythmic *legato* is interrupted by some jesting of the girls about Senta's infatuation with the portrait, and she is persuaded to sing them the Ballad of the Dutchman, which opens to a sea-call of 'Yo-ho-ho' to the Curse theme and continues with a melodic description of the ship with blood-red sails:

The sea-calls and whistling wind effects punctuate the song, and in the refrain we hear the theme of Senta's self-sacrifice already marked in the overture. At the end, the girl is so carried away that she ecstatically declares herself the one who will save the Dutchman from his doom.

It is at this moment that Erik, the young huntsman who has been more or less accepted as Senta's lover, enters and overhears her rapt declaration. He is as disturbed by it as Mary and the girls, who hasten away when he tells them Daland's ship is approaching the harbour.

Erik has another cause for distress: he knows his poverty is an obstacle in Daland's eyes to marriage with his daughter, and who, he asks, will plead for him if not Senta herself? The girl is in no mood to commit herself and rather waveringly asks if he doubts her devotion. When she tries to get away we have the kind of operatic duet so alien to the later Wagner and highly burlesquable at all times, both characters repeating their phrases *ad. lib.* to give rein to the music. It is, perhaps, difficult for the tenor in the circumstances to convey Wagner's image of a man "stormy, impulsive and gloomy, like every man who lives alone (particularly in the northern highlands)": had Wagner revised the opera as he intended we can imagine the wholly different kind of music he would have given Erik. The dream he relates in his fear of Senta's attachment to the Dutchman – in which he has seen her father bring the sinister mariner home and her sail with him to her doom – has greater atmosphere, and when he rushes away and Senta turns and finds herself face to face with Vanderdecken, whom her father has brought into the room, we have a characteristic Wagnerism – a long pause during which the pair gaze at each other, silent and rapt, their feelings conveyed only in the orchestra.

At last Senta forces herself to ask who the stranger is; and Daland describes the seaman's riches and wish to marry Senta in an *aria* of Italianate *fioritura*. Finding the two still speechless, he

Design by Helmut Jürgens for the Munich Opera of 'The Flying Dutchman', 1950

leaves them together, the horn intones the theme of the Curse, followed by Senta's 'self-sacrifice' on woodwind and horns, and the Dutchman begins the great duet of the opera, "*Wie aus der Ferne*", wonderingly commenting on this girl who seems to him like a vision of his possible saviour:

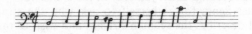

Senta radiantly brushes aside his doubts about her willingness to marry him, as her father wishes, if she really knew the cause of his need for redemption and the possible cost to herself: she proclaims her love to be changeless and given for life. It is not great music by Wagnerian standards, but it has some emotional force, although Daland's entrance brings in a Bellini-like jollity not truly in key.

The third act brings us back to the sea, where Wagner is always happiest in this opera. We are on the rocky shore by Daland's house, with the two ships in the background. The Norwegian sailors sing a rousing chorus and are joined in song and dance by a bevy of girls bringing them food and drink. The unlit silence of the Dutch ship attracts their attention, and a certain terror enters their gaiety as they hail the crew in vain. At last the Dutch sailors give a spectral response, the 'Yo-ho-ho!' of the Curse and a sinister chorus; a wind howls and whistles through their sails, and more terror strikes the Norwegians. They sing to revive their spirits, and are echoed in derisive laughter by the Dutch. At last they cross themselves in fear and go below.

Senta and Erik now appear, Erik again frightened and pleading with the girl: he sings an ardent *aria* in *cavatina* form which the Dutchman overhears. Believing Senta has already forgotten her promise, he rushes to his ship, while the girl tries vainly to undeceive him and Erik as desperately attempts to hold her back. The Dutchman pauses only to warn her darkly of the victims who have already suffered damnation by breaking faith with him, and in a pang of conscience tries to save her, despite his own agony, by revealing his true identity and leaping on board his ship, which puts to sea to his crew's ghostly chorus of the Curse. Now again a crowd has gathered on shore, but Senta breaks away from them and Erik and, protesting her unbroken faith and acceptance from the beginning of the Dutchman's identity, flings herself from the cliff into the sea. Immediately the Dutch ship sinks, and as the waves subside the figures of Senta and the Dutchman are seen rising in the sunset sky, locked in each other's arms.

In spite of the sentimental ending and unequal score – partly looking forward to Wagner's future, partly back into the operatic past – *The Flying Dutchman* was the opera that released Wagner for ever from thoughts of success in the material sense. The energy of his genius had been stimulated by the sea winds. From now onwards he knew he must follow a new and lonely musical star, whether the public could stumble after him or not. The next two operas were to bring him gradually in sight of his goal, and help to forge the master-creator of *Der Ring des Nibelungen* and its successors.

Tichatschek as Tannhaüser in the first performance, Dresden 1845

III Tannhäuser

Wagner appears to have first thought of composing an opera on the *Tannhäuser* myth through reading a pamphlet on the subject during his three years' sojourn in Paris. On his journey from Paris to Dresden, begun on the 7th of April, 1842, he visited Wartburg, traditional scene of the Song-Contest, and the visual impression made on him was so strong that three years later he was able to give the French scenic designer, Desplechin, a full description of the setting needed for the third act (a keen interest in design as well as production is something he may have inherited from Geyer, who began life as a painter before becoming an actor). The story of the knight who, on his way to the Wartburg Contest, succumbed to Venus and her worldly delights is a subject of German folk-song, and there are versions of the legend in Hoffmann's tales and elsewhere. But as usual Wagner correlated and invented material to such a degree that a completely new story emerged. The character of Elisabeth, and theme of redemption thereby made possible, were his own inventions, and it was, of course, natural to a musician to transform the poetry contest of the historical Minnesingers into one of song.

The opera was in many ways an advance on *The Flying Dutchman*, although its genesis from the earlier type of opera is still apparent in the fairly distinct *arias*, duets and *ensembles*. Nevertheless, Wagner was already developing a form of recitative and musical continuity which bears his own characteristic imprint (a comparison with the Mozartian or Beethovian form of recitative emphasises how great an individuality in this respect even the early Wagner shows), and the fact that the overture and Venusberg scenes were revised by the composer years later, after the composition of *Tristan und Isolde*, means the orchestral invention and colour reach at moments an altogether higher musical distinction than the opera as a whole. In fact, the overture – the last Wagner was to write with the sole exception of *Die Meistersinger** – is in some ways the opera's masterpiece, for it binds together all the superlative moments of the score in harmonic and instrumental variety and richness.

It opens softly, sombrely and majestically with the theme of the Pilgrim's Chorus on clarinets, valve horns and bassoons:

and after development overlaid with short descending phrases of the violins, brilliantly individual to this score, the religious themes merge into the theme associated with the Venusberg:

This is to all intents and purposes a key *motif* of the opera, for we hear it on a number of occasions during the action, including the contest in Act II and Tannhäuser's summoning of Venus in Act III: always when the knight's thoughts are concentrated on or pulling towards Venus. Nevertheless, the themes in *Tannhäuser* are not *leitmotifs* at all in the later sense of those in *The Ring*, for they are not musically developed or transformed but retain a

* From *Lohengrin* onwards it was replaced by a Prelude atmospheric to the theme of the opera.

fairly set character like those already in use by other opera composers. In no way is the score texture spun, as it were, out of *leitmotifs* – it is merely that a few of the melodies return later at appropriate dramatic moments.

Another melodic figure – below on oboe and clarinet beneath strings shimmering above the treble stave:

is characteristic of the Bacchanale, a dance in which Venus' evil and seductive followers expend their orgiastic frenzies. Both these last themes, with Tannhäuser's Hymn to Venus (heard first in the overture on a blare of trumpets in B major), are important contributions to the first act, but before this magnificent overture ends there are splendid new instrumental versions of the Pilgrim's Chorus and other themes, and the Venusberg music again forms a prelude to the first act after the rise of the curtain.

We are in a kind of grotto, abode of Venus, and as the goddess and her captive knight embrace we hear, like a soft echo, the exquisite and enticing chorus of the Sirens, the horn holding a sustained B beneath the silvery voices:

It recurs at the end of the frenzied dance of the Venusberg spirits, and seems suddenly to wake Tannhäuser from a dream that he dawningly realises is becoming a nightmare. In vain Venus attempts to dispel his rising longing for the earth. Momentarily she seems to succeed, and he plunges in feverish ecstasy into his panegyric, the Hymn to Venus:

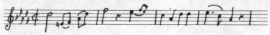

But it turns out to be a deceptive plea for release, despite her charms, and her soft enticements fail no less than her taunting fury: for she warns the knight that he will never escape her, but will long to return to the delights of love he is abandoning.

Nevertheless, his cry to Heaven releases him, Venusberg vanishes and the knight finds himself in the beautiful valley near the Wartburg known to him of old. It is spring, and the pipe of a shepherd-boy dances plaintively in the sunshine. It reminds us of the poignant *cor anglais* shepherd's tune at the opening of the third act of *Tristan*, and Puccini was to borrow the idea to set the distant rustic atmosphere in the beginning of Act III of *La Tosca*. In *Tannhäuser* it has a spring-like note, and the boy's song no overtones of tragedy. The pipe is still heard as the Pilgrims, tenors and basses, approach singing towards the hill path and Rome: their choruses are a blend of famous phrases, and we need only note here the haunting:

It is taken up by Tannhäuser himself in a cry of repentance that begs for divine mercy. The Pilgrims' chant dies away in the distance, and now hunting bugles are heard – three horns in F and three in E flat, echoing each other and heralding the entrance of the Landgrave and his followers. With them is Wolfram von Eschenbach, a minstrel, like Hans Sachs, based on an historical character (Wagner was reading a volume of his poems on a holiday in Marienbad in the summer of 1845, while waiting for the first *Tannhäuser* production at Dresden). He recognises Tannhäuser immediately and the knight has some uncomfortable moments trying to explain his long absence, which he vaguely puts down to foreign travel. His welcome, however, is moving and sincere, and he is deeply affected by Wolfram's hint that Elisabeth, the Landgrave's niece, has pined for him and will be happy at his return. Wolfram himself – the faithful, self-denying friend Wagner echoed in Kurwenal later – loves Elisabeth and already recognises, and is resigned to, his loss now Tannhäuser has returned. Her name:

45

← *Alexander Kipnis as the Landgrave*

Johanna Wagner as Elisabeth in the first performance of 'Tannhaüser', Dresden 1845

echoes on Tannhäuser's lips after Wolfram has pronounced it, and the theme interrupts the conventional choral Septet with which the act ends. It is to be heard again similarly in the third act during her funeral procession. Before the curtain falls, and as the Landgrave and his minstrels mount their horses, twelve horns hammer out a robust staccato tune curiously similar to one sued by Tchaikowsky in the second act hunting scene of *The Sleeping Beauty*.

46

Emmy Destinn as Elisabeth

The Introduction to the second act is a joyous theme which is, in fact, a prelude to Elisabeth's own outburst of joy when she enters the Hall of Song and greets it, radiant with the news of Tannhäuser's return.

It is the first and not the better of her two *arias*, but the happiness it conveys is infectious and enhances by contrast her later disappointments. A characteristic Wagnerian dramatic hush in the orchestra accompanies her meeting with Tannhäuser, brought in by Wolfram; he falls at her feet and is moved by her guileless revelation of her feelings. Their duet is conventionally operatic, like much of the music of this act, and the best Wagnerian invention throughout is in the instrumental punctuations, which can be dulcet and lovely, rather than the material given the singers. The phrase on the clarinet as Elisabeth watches the departing Tannhäuser and Wolfram:

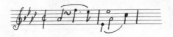

echoes the tune of the duet, and with underlining violins and cellos seems to give greater quality to the melody; but the flourish of the 'turn' is an old-fashioned device typical of much of the music – not only the soprano Elisabeth but even the bass and baritone, the Landgrave and Wolfram, resort to it.

After a melting moment between Elisabeth and the Landgrave, the minstrels enter for the contest, which is to be on the theme of love. Fanfares announce them, and the famous March theme is heard in both orchestra and four-part chorus:

Wolfram is the opening contestant, but his love song, though noble, seems cold and unrealistic to Tannhäuser, who has not yet thrown off his Venusberg passions. Indeed, as Venus warned, his background must still tragically betray him. He is not a particularly sympathetic character, too easily fluctuating between sacred and profane love and then lapsing into rather grovelling self-abasement: the great actor might make his suffering moving (hence Wagner's despairing search for a tenor capable of dramatically realising the character), but Wagner perhaps paints the lily in writing: "The essential features in Tannhäuser's character are his instant and complete absorption in the emotions caused by the circumstances of the moment, and the vivid contrasts produced in the expression of his feelings by any sudden change in the situation." Certainly Wolfram's chaste song provokes him into a more spirited assertion of physical love, and when the tenor Walther (a charming small part sometimes sung more gracefully than that of Tannhäuser) and dark-toned, angry Biterolf agree with Wolfram's conception, he loses his head and launches into the disastrous Hymn to Venus, tartly informing the outraged knights that they must experience such delights before they can pronounce adequately on the nature of love.

Only Elisabeth's intercession now saves Tannhäuser from being slain by the disturbed and pious singers on the theme of love*: her resisting cry of anguish for the man she still loves silences the tumult, and her melting phrases of appeal that Tannhäuser may yet be allowed to find forgiveness for his sin wins him the desired reprieve. He himself is softened and plunged into self-recrimination by her words, and accepts without question the Landgrave's decree that he shall make pilgrimage to Rome and seek absolution from the Pope.

To Wagner, dramatically, this was the key scene for Tannhäuser, though he could get no tenor to value it in comparison with the great dramatic Rome Narration of the third act. The crux, to the composer, was Tannhäuser's "*Zum Heil den Sündigen zu führen*", entreating salvation, and the culminating cry of "*Erbarm' dich mein!*" "The cries of '*Ach! erbarm' dich mein!*'", he wrote, "demand so poignant an accent that it is not sufficient here for him to be merely a well-trained singer; the highest dramatic art alone will endow him with the necessary energy of grief and des-

* If there is food for psychological thought here Wagner, thus early enamoured of the theme of sublimation of passion, does not pursue it.

peration for an expression that must seem to burst forth from the very bottom of a heart in the direst pain, like a cry for redemption. It is the conductor's duty to see that the desired effect is made possible to the chief singer by means of the most discreet accompaniment on the part of the rest of the voices and the orchestra." But the fact is the tenor proved usually too anxious to save his voice for the third act (despite Wagner's injunction to the Paris Tannhäuser, Albert Niemann: "In this act (i.e. Act III) I do *not* want any exhibition of sensuous power of voice... Everything is calculated here* in terms of a ghost-like tonelessness, with a gradual rise to no more than an expression of affecting softness"). It is true Wagner realised later that the overlay of chorus in the Act II *finale* made it difficult for Tannhäuser's essential cries to be adequately distinguished and make their full emotional effect. Often today he sings the whole passage unaccompanied, which at least settles the difficulty of his being heard.

The full *ensemble* then continues until the Chorus of Younger Pilgrims drifts up from the valley (almost too slickly on their dramatic cue), and with Tannhäuser's cry "To Rome!" and rush to join them, while Elisabeth and the knights echo his cry, the act ends.

The third act opens with a Prelude in which occurs a theme very similar to those suggesting the Grail in *Parsifal* and *Lohengrin*. Heard first *fortissimo* fading in *diminuendo*, it later takes on the silvery and mysterious sweetness, on four muted violins, which seems always in such themes to come in a form of mystic inspiration to Wagner:

It is followed here by first one and then two oboes, and a further passage on the flute. Later, we are to hear it as the 'Pardon' theme of Tannhäuser's Rome Narration. Wagner was always a master in the use of woodwind, and the beauty of this Prelude is a herald of the exquisitely delicate moments of religious sensibility he was to achieve in *Parsifal*, his last work. The inspiration never died, and without ever quite exactly repeating itself never changed its musical source across the years.

* Wagner was referring particularly to the Rome Narration.

50

As the curtain rises we are once again in the valley beneath the Wartburg; but it is now autumn, and sunset. Elisabeth is kneeling at a shrine, and Wolfram pauses in the forest path to watch her and muse mournfully on her grieving for Tannhäuser. Both start hopefully at a returning band of pilgrims from Rome, but although Elisabeth searches anxiously Tannhäuser is not among them. The tune of Elisabeth's Prayer, offering her life that Tannhäuser may be redeemed, is serene and candid like her whole personality:

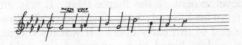

Sadly, on rising, she rejects Wolfram's offer to accompany her and passes from view. His *aria*, "O Star of Eve", is perhaps less moving than its recitative (the melodic invention of Wagner has not yet thrown off tradition and developed its own individual and lyric virtues). But the entry of Tannhäuser, weary, ragged, and leaning on his staff, brings a finer note into the score, and we hear again a hint of the Venusberg Bacchanale.

Wolfram fears he has never been to Rome, but Tannhäuser in his long and sombre Narration bitterly tells of his journey there – mortifying himself with hardships in his search for redemption – only at the end to be refused absolution: never can his sin be forgiven, until the barren staff has put forth flowers or leaves. The sad, echoing instrumental punctuation of this Narration is characteristic of it:

Desperate and hopeless, and against all Wolfram's entreaties, the knight vows he will return to Venus, and at his call she does appear in fleeting vision, accompanied by fragments of the Venus music and Chorus of Sirens. But at Wolfram's cry of "Elisabeth" Tannhäuser is mentally dragged back to the world, the vision vanishes, and from the distance floats a chorus telling of the death of Elisabeth. When the pilgrims enter bearing her body, Tann-

51

UNIVERSITY OF ILLINOIS
MUSIC LIBRARY

häuser falls by the bier in exhaustion and grief: and as he dies the pilgrims take his staff, now bursting into leaf as a sign of divine mercy. Elisabeth's intercession has brought death to the body, but life to the soul.

Much of this today is against religious feeling and taste: nor musically does the work take the place it once did in the Wagner *canon*. But that Wagner's personal feeling about the struggle of sacred and profane love, and the capacity of the noble to conquer the degrading, was sincere is shown by his mature and increasingly mystical development of the theme later. It was an instinct inseparable from his life and work, which musically flowered like the staff at the end of this early opera. It was his tragedy that *Tannhäuser* was widely heard and conquered the public only years after he had, as a composer, left it far behind, and in the study developed an altogether more revolutionary form of music-drama, revealing the infinitely greater stature of his mature genius. And of this tragedy he himself was only too bitterly aware.

'Siegfrieds Tod': fragment of orchestral score

Nun sei bedankt, mein lieber Schwan
Zieh durch die weite Fluth zurück
Dahin, woher mich trug dein Kahn,
Kehr' wieder nur ... zum Glück!

Lohengrin

von Wagner

IV   Lohengrin

In *Lohengrin* Wagner came to the end of an operatic phase, and at the same time reached out to his great and mature music-drama period. The leading *motifs* are here used altogether more seriously and flexibly than in *Tannhäuser*, and although the choral links in the narrative glow splendidly in something of the old tradition of part-writing and vocal harmony, the integration of the score is closer than in any opera yet. The continuity of the music pattern anticipates *The Ring*, and the mystical content of the story inspired Wagner to new wonders of composition in the orchestra, divorced as it were from the flesh and sounding a spiritual note only fragmentarily touched on in *Tannhäuser*.

The romantic opera in *Lohengrin* reached its zenith; and although its debt to Weber's *Euryanthe* is obvious – particularly in the opposition of a bright (Lohengrin and Elsa) and dark couple (Telramund and Ortrud) – its mystical ancestor is more truly Mozart's *Magic Flute*. But in *Lohengrin*, where librettist and musician are one, an entirely new form of music-drama emerges, in which poetry of idea and dramatic construction are fused with the music to a degree impossible where two minds (and the librettist's an inferior one) try to create a coherent whole. *Lohengrin* looks forward to *Parsifal*, Wagner's last work, and not only because of its common thematic connection with the Grail legend (Lohengrin, as we learn at the end of this opera, is Parsifal's son).

The psychology in *Lohengrin* also shows, far more than in *Tannhäuser*, Wagner's gift, supreme in *The Ring* and his later operas, of humanising legendary material so that it becomes symbolic of the forces of character and conscience that are at the heart

55

of civilised literature and human experience. The tale of the Swan Knight is embodied in Danish and Anglo-Saxon legends of the Skiff ("Sceaf") and in the four Mabinogion myths of Irish-occupied Wales. This Celtic background was also a force in the creation of the legends of King Arthur and his Knights of the Round Table, from which the story of the Holy Grail (the wine-cup used by Christ at the Last Supper, and in which Joseph of Arima-thea caught the drops of blood from Christ's wound on the Cross) derives. In later legends the home of the Grail shifts to Montsalvat in the Spanish Pyrenees, where the guardians of the Grail are knights whose mediaeval chivalry still takes the form of journeying to succour the innocent and oppressed. Parsifal (sometimes called Perceval) is chief guardian of the Grail, and it is his son who comes to help Elsa in her distress.

Mingled with these stories is the even older myth (dating back to the Greek legend of Semele) of the immortal who loves a mortal, but is tragically forced to return to his or her spiritual world when the loved one proves unable to sustain love on the higher plane, without human error. This was the Romantic Period legend of Undine the water-nymph, well known to Wagner who was greatly attracted by it. This conflict of soul between the divine and the failing human Wagner brought to a new psychological poignancy in his Lohengrin and Elsa; and his drawing of Telramund, too, shows original currents of feeling, conscience and maddened pride in the operatic villain. Finally, he bound the story together with the symbolic background of a different kind of conflict: the conflict of Christianity with the pagan world it was superseding, and of whose gods Ortrud is here a last despairing (and in this sphere quite sincere) priestess. Her witchcraft and superstition are the Dark Ages opposite to the growing brightness and power of the Christian faith.

The Prelude that precedes *Lohengrin*, unlike the normal overture which binds together all the principal melodies of an opera, is a concentrated essence of one theme, the Holy Grail, and therefore of the mystical background of the whole story:

← *Kirsten Flagstad as Elsa*

It first appears high above the treble stave on divided violins, achieves a gradual crescendo through woodwind, violas, cellos and horns to a burnished climax of trumpets and trombones, and then fades mysteriously to silence on muted violins, supplemented by flutes in the soft chords just before the end. In the last three bars the theme is repeated in an exquisite *pianissimo* on the violins, creating an effect of unearthly radiance like the light around the Grail itself.

The scene opens in a meadow by the banks of the Scheld near Antwerp, in the time of King Henry the Fowler (tenth century), who is about to start a campaign against the invading Hungarians. He and his knights are gathered on the river bank, and a Herald (not an inconspicuous baritone rôle) opens the proceedings to the martial *motif* of the King's Call. The King himself, a noble expo-

'Lohengrin': setting for Act I, Covent Garden

nent of Germanic aims in the Wagnerian tradition, in a long
monologue shows concern not merely at the military situation,
but at that in the territory of Brabant where they are gathered;
and he asks Frederick of Telramund to explain the apparent
disunity in the state, so disruptive at a time of war.

Telramund, as the King makes clear, is a knight known for
valour and honour, and his story causes sharp consternation
rather than immediate disbelief. He claims that the boy ruler of
Brabant, Gottfried, of whom the late Duke had left him the
guardian, has been spirited into the forest and slain by his sister
Elsa, in a sinister design to claim the throne for herself and her
lover. During his narrative he makes the interesting admission
that he had, until then, desired to marry Elsa, but in repugnance at

her deed and the discovery that she had a lover (whose identity he cannot give) he had married instead Ortrud, princess of a race who had once ruled in Brabant. This dark, proud beauty he presents to the King: but later in his narrative he slips into the truth – that Elsa had, in fact, rejected his advances. Several psychological factors, therefore, are at work in Telramund, destroying his former character, the 'man scorned' being one of them. But as we do learn later, he is not wholly aware of his subconscious motives (which certainly include personal ambition), and genuinely believes his story of the murder which his wife – a pretended eye-witness from the palace tower – has told him. In fact the boy heir has disappeared through Ortrud's witchcraft, and been transformed by her into a swan.

The King, only half-believing in the guilt of the gentle girl, prays for divine wisdom and orders her to come for trial. Her entrance with her women is marked by her own *motif*, resigned and serene:

and is preceded by a lovely falling melody on oboes and *cor anglais* which is also associated with her:

Her head is downcast, and to Telramund's denunciations and the King's questions she seems strangely impervious, singing only of a dream in which she still appears to be moving, the vision of a knight who will appear to champion her:

The Grail *motif* sounding in her Dream narration tells us the knight is Lohengrin, and his characteristic *motif* appears beneath her voice:

It will be heard much later, and at the end of the opera in minor key. But the call of the trumpets twice fails to bring the champion to the combat with Telramund which shall decide the issue. Then at last, to choral excitement, he is glimpsed in the distance: a knight in shining armour, gliding down the curving river in a boat drawn by a swan. It is to this swan, as he lands, that he addresses the serenely charming farewell, always to be associated with it:

He is greeted with respect by the King, and as Elsa has already in her prayer promised her hand to her champion should he wish it, he asks her if she will be his wife. It is no mere formality: and we have cause soon to realise how deeply the unworldly knight has been affected by the girl in distress, and feels an idyllic promise of happiness with a companion who can assuage the loneliness of one from a world of dedication, outside normal human relationships. But there is a warning and a fear: never must the woman ask his name and the place from which he came. The Grail must preserve its secret, and its messengers must always be anonymous –

Lauritz Melchior as Lohengrin

once the secret is revealed the emissary must return to Montsalvat, and renounce human contact. Elsa, of course, does not know this, and tragedy for them both must spring from it; but at the moment she is too overjoyed to seek reasons, and radiantly promises both her silence and her hand.

Lohengrin's warning, though, is to permeate the score: solemn, noble and beautiful, it has the hint of tragedy to come:

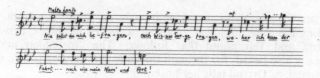

The shining melody of Elsa's reply, rapt at the beauty of her deliverer, is also by contrast to throw pathos on her uncertainty later:

The chorus tend to share her faith, but Telramund furiously refuses to yield without a fight, and is soon unarmed by the radiant stranger, who spares his life. Elsa again has a tune of lyrical and uminous beauty, hailing Lohengrin's victory:

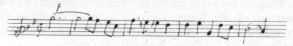

but in the ecstatic *ensemble* which magnificiently ends the act the darker thread of Ortrud's vengeful voice is heard for the first time.

In the second act, crouched with her brooding, broken husband on the Cathedral steps in the citadel of Antwerp, her evil personality begins fully to assert itself. In the sombre Prelude we have already heard on the cellos two *motifs*, closely associated, which are to be the dark psychological force in Elsa's betrayal – the *motifs* representing Ortrud's plotting and the "doubt" of Lohengrin which she plans to instil in the young girl's mind:

(a)

(b)

We are to hear them sound ominously on future occasions, including the long duologue, in the shadows of the night, between Ortrud and Telramund that follows. The "forbidden name" theme is also heard: for through this only can Lohengrin and Elsa be parted, as Ortrud tells her husband.

Telramund has been wrapped in rage, hurt pride (for he values his reputation as a knight) and despair, and his rage does not spare his wife whose truth about Elsa's crime he begins to suspect. She does, in fact, by her plan divert his anger and raise his hopes, and in his weakness and misery he is eager enough to believe her confident assertion that Lohengrin overcame him by sorcery – thus ascribing the black magic she practises to her Christian foe. In some respects Telramund invokes pity, and though more ruthless and passionate he is psychologically a forerunner of Wagner's later victim of another's evil, Gunther in *Götterdämmerung* – as the fine artist and most intelligent actor-singer of both parts, Hermann Uhde, has demonstrated in our time.

The unhappiness of the banished couple has not been softened by the sounds of music from the nearby Pallas of the knights, but when Elsa, on the night before her wedding, appears on the moonlit balcony of the Kemenate (or women's dwelling) Ortrud is ready with her plan. An exquisite soft phrasing on the clarinets, following one on the flutes, preludes Elsa's song:

It is one of Wagner's sweet and ethereal contrasts: candid and true after the dark dramatic scene between the scheming couple on the steps below. The guileless girl is easily enough lured into pity by Ortrud's appeal to her and assertion of her innocence, while Telramund disappears into the shadows to try and rally some

Leonie Rysanek as Elsa in Wieland Wagner's production of 'Lohengrin' at Bayreuth, 1958

disaffected knights to his side. And as she descends to offer shelter to her disgraced and now ragged enemy, she does not hear Ortrud's passionate invocation of her heathen gods which is as splendid as it is virulent. The net indeed has a bigger fish than Elsa to enmesh: Christianity itself must be wiped out by a restoration of the pagan religion. And before Elsa has guided her enemy with compassion into the Kemenate, Ortrud has already instilled the first doubt – the suggestion that Lohengrin's magic may not be divine but the reverse: a hint the girl easily rejects in her first glow of happiness, but which is to return to trouble her mind later.

65

The coming of dawn is heralded by trumpets from the tower and the remote distance, echoing each other in one of Wagner's typically striking martial effects. After a strong chorus, the Herald sings the official proclamation of Telramund's banishment, and of Lohengrin's intention after his wedding to lead the Brabantian army against the invaders. The bridal procession of women follows:

But as Elsa moves to join Lohengrin on the Cathedral steps, Ortrud, unable in her jealous pride to sustain her mask of contrition, imperiously flings herself before her rival on the steps and claims her own precedence. Once again in Elsa's ears there sounds the suggestion of Lohengrin's unknown background, and now Telramund's dramatic accusation of black magic against her bridegroom; and her momentary hesitation gives pathos to Lohengrin's angry demand to Ortrud to keep away from her, and appeal to Elsa's own faith. For him, too, there is uncertainty and fear: he wins Elsa to him quickly enough and tenderly leads the distressed girl into the Cathedral; but Ortrud, confident in her poison, remains menacingly undisturbed before the fury of the nobles, and as Elsa glances back she sees her gesture of triumphant defiance, as the 'forbidden name' *motif* blazes in the brass.

The third act is heralded by a joyous prelude, and the chorus that accompanies the leading of the young couple into the bridal chamber has become a regular accompaniment to weddings:

It is hardly the highest artistic point in the score, and its affinity to the *Tannhäuser* march manner may be explained by the fact that Wagner composed the music of this act before that of Acts I and II.

Nevertheless, when Elsa and Lohengrin, shy in their happiness, are left alone together, their duet has many beauties of a rather Italianate style:

But Lohengrin's tender speaking of her name only reminds Elsa of the sad and rather frightening fact that she still does not know his own. Clinging to his hope of human happiness, and love for her, he tries to turn her mind to other things, and leads her gently to the window, drawing her attention to the sweet scent of the flowers outside. But Elsa's fears are by now irrevocably mixed with a passionate desire to share her husband's secret and perhaps help him: it is her own love and generosity, the will to give, that betray her. The mystic note in her nature that had drawn Lohengrin to her aid also reasserts itself to her ruin: in a distraught vision she sees the swan coming, as she fears, to draw Lohengrin away from her, and not all his anguished yet tender warnings can now stop her distracted demand that he put her mind at rest by telling her the truth, now, at once, before her marriage is wrecked by the constant terror of losing him.

The fatal question cannot now be stalled; and even as Lohengrin realises, in despair, that he has lost her, she hears a sound outside and thrusts his sword into his hand just as Telramund and his murderous followers dramatically burst into the chamber. Lohengrin kills his assailant instantly; and, deeply shocked, stands numb and silent until he can bring himself to the brief fatal admission that their happiness is forever lost. Tender with Elsa still, and to the poignant phrases of the love duet, he raises the fainting girl and places her on a couch; but to her cry to heaven for pity he can only sadly announce that she must dress herself to appear before the King and Court, when he will reveal his secret and depart. We hear again the permeating *motif* of the forbidden name: then the scene changes to the meadow of the first act, where the nobles assemble to the fanfares of trumpets in E flat, D and F.

King and knights are preparing for battle, unaware of tragedy until the appearance of a pale and downcast Elsa reveals to them that something is seriously amiss. Lohengrin is hailed with joy, which is quickly quenched by his solemn announcement that he can no longer lead them: Elsa's broken promise forces him to reveal his secret and return to the distant land from which he came. His Narration, *In fernem Land*, gravely evokes the image of Montsalvat and the story of the Holy Grail and its dedicated knights:

The music is dulcet and he himself mystically rapt, until the final revelation of his name, Lohengrin, swells to a trumpet crescendo. Sadly he takes farewell of the grieving Elsa, whose appeals are vainly supported by those of the King and chorus. And his decision is reinforced by the appearance of the swan, to a *motif* (on violins in four parts) we are to hear again in the first act of *Parsifal*:

He greets it to the tune of his farewell in the first act, and his calm resignation is broken by a pang of anguish at the thought that in a year Elsa, now lost to him, could, through his aid, perhaps have been reunited with her vanished brother. He leaves with her his horn, sword and ring in case the boy should be found; but as he steps into the boat Ortrud breaks from the throng and claims the swan is Gottfried himself – the chain around the bird's neck was placed there by herself, holding him in bondage. Lohengrin now sinks to his knees in prayer, and as the white dove of the Grail hovers over his head rises and, in inspiration, unfastens the chain. The swan sinks and Lohengrin lifts to the bank the youth Gottfried, Elsa's brother. Then, as Elsa and the nobles greet the boy in incredulous joy, he quietly sails away, his head bent in speechless sorrow over his shield.

Elsa, turning and finding him gone, cries out in desperation for her husband, and sinks lifeless in the arms of her brother. She has paid the price of the mortal who loves a being from another world, yet cannot rise above her human fears and limitations. That he has paid the price, too, in a loneliness that has proved unconquerable by human love, is the key to the tragedy and pathos of Wagner's opera.

Hermann Uhde as Telramund

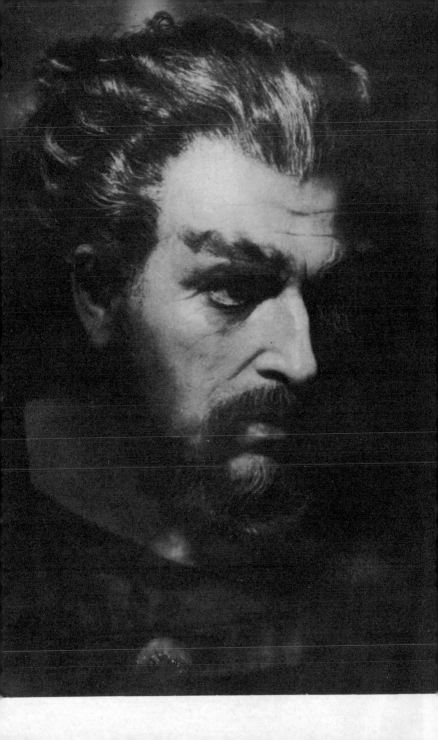

V Der Ring des Nibelungen

The composition of *The Ring*, poems and music, occupied Wagner over a span of twenty-six years. It was in the summer of 1848 that he first showed his interest in the Nibelungen myth through the publication of two essays, and in November the same year he completed his first dramatic poem on the subject, *Siegfrieds Tod*. But the deeper he became involved in the inspiration of the theme, the more it became apparent to him that the story of Siegfried's death needed clarification and expansion: its roots were in the past, the need for the hero to free humanity from the domination of the Gods, themselves tainted by mortal sins and conscience, arose from dramatic threads too complex to stand alone in one final tragedy. *Siegfried*, *Die Walküre* and finally *Das Rheingold*, the prelude to the saga, therefore sprang to life poetically until the whole narrative spread over four operas, of which *Siegfrieds Tod*, later transformed into *Götterdämmerung*, was the last. The music, unlike the librettos, was composed chronologically and it was not until the 21st of November, 1874, when the Bayreuth Festival was in active preparation, that Wagner completed the last note of *Götterdämmerung*.

All this explains a certain amount of repetitive narrative in the music-dramas which Wagner was never entirely able to eliminate (although it has its explanatory uses when the operas are performed, not in a cycle, but singly). And it must be realised for full artistic appreciation that the poems, written in Wagner's highly individual literary style and vocabulary, are an integral part of the music, which in many cases was already beating in his brain as he

← *'Die Walküre': Hans Hotter as Wotan*

wrote them. The fabric of words and music was with him creatively intertwined to a degree that in effect turned opera into a new form, the music-drama, and his use of the *leitmotif*, which came to its zenith in *The Ring*, was an endlessly rich and varied way of expressing ideas as well as characters in music.

Beethoven's symphonies had given some indication of a musical texture in which melody is interrupted rather than prolonged; but Wagner carried the tendency much further, and revolutionised opera by introducing symphonic orchestration which played at least as large a part as the voices in the development of the full score. As a result the *aria*, although it seems to blaze spasmodically as a link in the orchestral chain (Siegmund's Spring Song is a case in point), virtually disappeared as a separate entity, and his melodic themes wove themselves into a continuous structure in which their repetitions, with infinite changes of modulation and tone colour, and shifts among the various instruments, became a descriptive essence of the drama itself; often so graphically indicating the nature of a character's thought that his words are almost superfluous.

It is, however, an error to deduce from this a lack of melody: very often, it is true, the thematic tune is in the orchestra rather than the voice, and the singer is allotted a form of recitative known as *Sprechgesang*; but this itself demands melodious delivery and Wagner was highly sensitive to the need for this. It was still *bel canto* he required in singing, but a German *bel canto* able to adapt itself to the inter-relation of the vocal and orchestral line, and also to the needs of the drama in a way rare in operatic singers. The fact that melody in his later works became equally divided between orchestra and singers did not affect this basic effect of melodiousness in his scores, nor the demands of pure singing from his singers. The demands are not always met; but the greatest Wagnerian artists have always met them in addition to the often stupendous acting needs.

As a dramatist Wagner dealt in symbols, to an extent, which he merged with the Shakespearean humanities: the myth, therefore, as a basis of plot always attracted him. Both German and Icelandic sagas on the Nibelungen race and Siegfried contributed to the plot and characters of *The Ring*; but as was the way with Shakespeare, working on ready-made materials, Wagner's genius re-formed and dramatised them until they were shaped into new works with new psychological and moral foundations. Nowhere is this clearer than in his characterisation of Wotan, chief of the

Gods, who becomes the basic tragic figure in the cycle, as important as Siegfried himself, a symbol of power abused and therefore superseded. And the stolen gold from the Rhine turns the whole work into a great sociological allegory: an allegory of greed for gold, the disastrous consequences of this and of the abnegation of love it involves, and the enormities of slave labour (Alberich and the Nibelungen) that accompany the drive for power.

It was this side of the drama, of course, that interested Bernard Shaw, who in *The Perfect Wagnerite* describes also the basic Wagnerian conception in *The Ring* of "love as the fulfiller of our Will to Live and consequently our reconciler to night and death". The cosmic cataclysm of the last act of *Götterdämmerung* he could not accept, and indeed, although dramatically it was a natural apex of the tragedy, Wagner himself took some time to work it out and showed a certain distrust of it outside its magnificent theatrical effect.

'Das Rheingold': setting by Leslie Hurry for Covent Garden, 1954

'*Das Rheingold*': *The entry of the Gods into Valhalla.*

New production by Wolfgang Wagner, Bayreuth, 1960.

Das Rheingold

Das Rheingold, the opening key to the drama, begins in the depths of the river Rhine, where three Rhinemaidens swim round the gold embedded in the rock: treasure which is the source of material power and the whole subsequent tragedy. Fashioned into a ring, it will give supreme dominance to whoever wears it; but at the same time its theft will bring tragedy upon the world and all who own the ring. Only its return to the Rhine can divert that tragedy and bring peace back to the earth.

Its theft, and the first repercussions of that tragedy, are the basis of this opening drama in the cycle. But before that becomes apparent the music itself carries us deep below the Rhine into a mysterious world of shadowy waters, suggesting the image of existence before the creation of the earth and coming of man. Its centrifugal point is the chord of E flat major, sustained miraculously through many bars and orchestral mutations: at first as a single low note, so soft as to suggest not only depth but a world of silence; then supplemented at the fifth bar by its fifth, and later by the gradually rising, wave-like undulations of the river itself. Below are three forms of the development:

75

The idea for this Prelude came to Wagner in a kind of waking dream in a hotel at Spezia, and its poetic aptness suggests, indeed, that creative inspiration that is beyond the craftsman's analysis. "The rush and roar", wrote Wagner, "soon took musical shape within my brain as the chord of E flat major, surging incessantly in broken chords: these declared themselves as melodic figurations of increasing motion, yet the pure triad of E flat major never changed, but seemed by its steady persistence to impart infinite significance to the element in which I was sinking. I awoke from my half-sleep in terror, feeling as though the waves were now rushing high above my head. I at once recognised that the orchestral prelude to *The Rhinegold*, which for a long time I must have carried about within me, yet had never been able to fix definitely, had at last come to being in me: and I quickly understood the very essence of my own nature: the stream of life was not to flow to me from without, but from within."

This pervasive music imagery of the primaeval river is to echo in many later *motifs* associated with it (the Rhinemaidens, the Rhinegold, Thunder, the Fall of the Gods, the Sword, the Ride of the Valkyries, Brünnhilde's Sleep, all are coloured to an extent by its rhythm and rising melody), and it is to be notably repeated in *Götterdämmerung*, the climax of the drama here begun. It is the first indication of that musical identification with Nature that caused Gabriel Monod, writing of *The Ring* at the first Bayreuth Festival, to exclaim: "You feel you are in the presence of a force of nature, unleashing itself with almost reckless violence."

The shimmering quietness of the depths of the Rhine moves to a *crescendo* of swirling water; and the Rhinemaidens begin their characteristic song above the musical motion of the waves:

Their carefree and seductive tones (to become plaintive later) attract the attention of Alberich, the Nibelung dwarf, who is fascinated by the maidens swimming and playing in the green waters and, as he clambers clumsily after them,* learns the story of the gold that they are guarding. They laugh at his grotesque attempts

* Wagner does not explain why the Nibelung is amphibious, and unfortunately for him Hagen, Alberich's son, proves not to have inherited the quality at the end of *Götterdämmerung*.

76

to woo them; and feeling his incapacity to inspire love, his evil nature becomes centred on the power the gold can bring. The Rhinegold *motif* echoes softly, at first, as the maidens sing its praises; and its beauty, suddenly revealed in the flickering light, burns itself into the dwarf's covetous brain:

Only one of its guardians, Flosshilde, realises the danger; but Alberich by now, from the taunting Woglinde and Wellgunde, has learned too much and, lusting for power, renounces the love he can never know,

and, clambering up the rock, seizes the gold as the terrified Rhine-maidens scatter with dolorous cries. Light leaves the Rhine in an eternal night, and Alberich's mocking laughter echoes as the river-music dissolves into the Ring *motif*, which is to pervade the whole cycle:

Das Rheingold is continuous in performance, and the waves change into clouds and mist which part to reveal the second scene. We are on the mountain heights, with Wotan and the sleeping Fricka, his wife and queen, resting on a plateau with the sky and the great new Palace of Valhalla, which the Giants have just built as a fortress for the Gods, behind them. The Ring *motif* wanes and by Wagner's miraculous powers of musical transformation and

77

mutability is merged into the new and dominating theme of Valhalla, majestic, serene and glorious in the key of D flat major:

Here in 3/4 time, moulded in brass, it is to recur in many other keys, tempi and instrumental combinations, one of its most impressive transformations occurring in *Siegfried*, Act III, Scene 1, when it is woven into a splendid four-time fabric with the *motif* of the Sword as the basic thread:

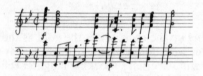

Wotan's craving for power is as yet unconnected with the Ring, but has expressed itself through this architectural vision which has been achieved only by a fatal Treaty with the Giants, Fafner and Fasolt, written indelibly on Wotan's symbol of authority, his spear. For their services the brothers have claimed Freia, Fricka's sister, the Goddess of Youth and Beauty on whose golden apples the Gods depend for their immortality. Wotan, inspired by the wily diplomacy of Loge, the strange inconstant God of Fire, has every hope of evading the terms of this Treaty: it is the first great crack in the edifice of his character, and the god-like ideal.

Through much of this opera and the next the Treaty *motif* pervades his thoughts:

We hear it almost at once, a solemn descent which is the root, too, later of the Dejection *motif* of Wotan (sometimes called his "Rage"); a mood of gloom springing from the results of this dishonoured Treaty.

At the moment Fricka is the more worried of the two, and her fears are not stilled when Freia enters in flight from the Giants. Theirs is a menacing, sombre theme, rhythmically suggesting their heavy tread and the impact of their great staves with the ground: Titans of the earth:

There is nothing impersonal about them. Fasolt is rather touchingly mellowed by the thought of Freia gracing their cold hearth, and it is Fafner, the more reticent of the two at first, whose thoughts are set impregnably on the Treaty and the realisation of the waning vitality Freia's loss will mean to the Gods. Donnor, God of Thunder, and Froh, God of Spring, brothers of Freia, try and intervene when the Giants, feeling Wotan is tricking them, seize their sister, but Wotan stretches out his spear in token of honour, while secretly deeply anxious about Loge's failure to appear and find the promised solution.

The flicker of mounting flames heralds his approach:

and this *motif* personal to Loge is closely followed by another of the 'Flames' Spell':

Although he only appears in this one opera, Loge's trickery, elusive as fire, is to be recalled on many occasions later, notably in the superb Fire Music at the climax of *Die Walküre*, where again we are to hear these two themes in association. He is a being apart from the Gods, without allegiance; his insinuating tenor as individual as Wagner's description of his stage figure: "Face pale and shining, eyes large and black and intensified by silver foil: his hair a light red, and erect like twisted flames."

He describes now how he had roamed the world in search of ransom for Freia, but could find nothing man would prefer to the love of a woman. He also narrates the story of the Rhinegold, and of Alberich who has renounced love to gain it. The passions he arouses in his listeners – greed and lust for power – are all part of his cunning purpose: he is a Puck of the sky, the wreaker of mischief. The Giants agree to renounce Freia in exchange for the Nibelung gold, and carry her off as hostage.

Already the Gods seem to grow older: a mist rises, and Wotan, now desperate, descends with Loge into the dark cavernous world of the Nibelungen. Here we find Alberich in gloating domination, the power of the gold having turned his people into his slaves. After an orchestral interlude in which the semi-quaver flicker of Loge's fire theme merges with other *motifs*, we hear the hammer-on-anvil rhythm of the Nibelungen Forge, always an indication of the world of the enslaved dwarfs:

And with it the Rhinegold fanfare shows us that Alberich has already forged the Ring.

His immediate concern is the magic Tarnhelm which he is bullying his brother Mime, the smith, to produce: it is a helmet or cap which will enable its wearer to become invisible. Its *motif* is one of mysterious and sinister beauty:

Mime, forced to give up his prize, is discovered howling by Wotan and Loge and is easily beguiled into telling the whole tale. Alberich, returning with his slaves and the hoard of gold, and driving

80

all away with his outstretched hand on which is the Ring of power, is a greater obstacle to Loge's cunning; but his vanity defeats him. He is persuaded to turn himself into a dragon by the aid of the Tarnhelm. Loge, cowering in apparent fear, nevertheless suggests it would be more difficult to change into something really small. Alberich responding with a toad, he is easily overcome and triumphantly borne away to Valhalla, to another orchestral interlude dominated by the hammering Nibelung anvils.

As the Gods return, the mist around Valhalla clears, and Alberich is forced to summon the Nibelungs to bring the hoard of gold. In a gnome-like flurry they deposit the gold and scatter like grey mice back to their subterranean abode. Alberich still hopes to retain the Ring, but in a great scene of conflict with Wotan it is Wotan who tears it from his finger, and by retaining it succumbs himself to the temptations, and the moral Nemesis, of power. He, now, bears the burden of the theft of the gold (Rhinegold fanfare in the orchestra), and also of Alberich's thundered, despairing Curse on the Ring and all who own it:

In this moment the dwarf gains stature, a formidable and commanding Lucifer. As, raging with revengeful laughter, he returns to the underworld, Fasolt and Fafner reappear with Freia. The Gods revive, as the blocks of gold are piled up to hide Freia: this is the Giants' stipulation, and they are not satisfied until both Tarnhelm and Ring are added to conceal the last glint of her eye – although Wotan only parts with the Ring after a supreme self-struggle, and after advice from Erda, all-wise goddess of the earth, who rises from its depths to help him face the crisis.

Nevertheless, he is not freed from the Curse: he has committed himself, and not returned the gold to the Rhine. And the Curse itself works quickly: Fafner slays his brother to gain possession of the gold. We are to meet him again in *Siegfried*, guarding his stolen hoard in the form of a Dragon whom Siegfried, the hero and human redeemer, must slay.

As Donner with his great hammer invokes the thunder:

and the rainbow appears as a bridge across the sky along which the Gods can approach Valhalla, we hear another theme close to Siegfried, the Sword *motif* which is to echo through *Die Walküre:*

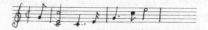

It is here merely an idea forming in Wotan's mind – an idea to which Erda has contributed. From this idea are to spring the army of the Valkyrie, daughters of Wotan and Erda who guard Valhalla, and the tragic race of the Wälsungs who come from his association with a human woman. Already in his mind there stirs the thought of Siegmund, his unborn Wälsung son, and, though as yet unknown to him, Siegfried, his grandson, the hero without fear or corruption who must free humanity from the tainted rule of the Gods, and make man the master of his own destiny.

In the meantime Wotan's noble and expanding vocal line reminds us only of the grandeur of the God; the Gods enter Valhalla in majestic procession, the orchestra full blaze. Only Loge lags behind, contemptuously disassociating himself from their guessed-at doom. And across the grandeur cuts the plaintive song of the Rhinemaidens, bewailing Wotan's treachery. The last word is with them – grieving, yet also a threat.

Die Walküre

In *Die Walküre* we are for the first time on the earth and among human inhabitants: and Wotan's "idea" at the end of *Das Rheingold* has taken shape in Brünnhilde, his favourite daughter by Erda, and her eight sisters, the Valkyrie, who, riding the skies on their wild horses, bring the bodies of slain heroes to Valhalla to guard it from the Nibelung hordes. But it is the human beings born of the "idea" – the tragic Wälsungs – whom we meet first, the twin brother and sister, Wotan's children, who have been named Siegmund and Sieglinde, and now meet, unconscious of their identity, for the first time since early childhood.

As in *Rheingold* we are conscious first of the forces of Nature: not the flowing underwater world of the Rhine but the thunder and lightning of the raging storms about the earth. The orchestral prelude is ominous and agitated (*furioso* in the score and waxing and waning in tempest-like alternations of *forte* and *piano*):

The Thunder *motif* pierces it, before the storm dies down and the curtain rises on the first scene, Hunding's hut in the forest. "A great ash-tree rises from the centre", in Wagner's directions: in it, invisible as yet, is embedded the sword which Wotan, appearing unrecognised on Sieglinde's wedding night, has thrust into the trunk and which only Siegmund, the destined hero, will be able to release.

The door of the hut flies open and Siegmund, exhausted by storm and flight, staggers into the flickering firelight and collapses by the hearth. We have heard the *motif* of his Fatigue:

Lotte Lehmann as Sieglinde

and now, with the entry of Sieglinde, another gentle melody in melting thirds winds itself into our hearts and is to be associated with her many times later. It expresses her compassion at the pitiful state of the hunted stranger:

Frida Leider as Brünhilde

They are to interweave with others which form the fabric of their story: for as she ministers to him and brings him food they eye each other strangely, two blonde creatures already sensitive to their as yet unrevealed relationship. And the orchestra lingers on the theme of Siegmund's Flight and the bond of Love which grows from it: for it has brought him to Sieglinde's house:

These themes are to be the lyrical foundation of the whole exquisite duet which recurs between the pair in this act, a luminous texture of love and devotion poignant in its short-lived ecstasy.

But first Sieglinde must tell the stranger that the hut belongs to her husband, Hunding; and as they sip in turn from the horn of mead, and are bound in a wondering silence, the orchestra spins out shining threads of tentative feeling. Cellos pierce sadly through the fabric, and Siegmund's face and voice darken as he describes how misfortune follows him: "*Wehwalt hiess ich mich selbst*" ("Woeful have I been called"). He fears to bring disaster on Sieglinde, but she persuades him gently to await Hunding's coming and, weaponless as he is, claim hospitality for the night. And as she does so we hear for the first time the lamenting theme of the tragic Wälsung race:

It is rudely interrupted by the menacing horn of Hunding and his theme:

a magnificent stroke of dramatic and character contrast of the kind of which Wagner is a master.

Hunding is as threatening and as dark in appearance as his music: armed with shield and spear, he gives them to Sieglinde and orders her to prepare a meal. Meanwhile, he eyes the stranger with morose curiosity. The music tells us he has noticed the likeness of the brother and sister – including the snake-like glint of the eyes which is ascribed in the sagas to the Wälsung race. He demands to know Siegmund's story and reluctantly the Wälsung describes his background – how he had lived as a child with his father, Wolfe, and mother and sister in the forest; how the mother had been killed by marauding enemies and the sister carried off by them; and how he and his father had lived wildly in the woods after

86

finding the charred remains of their home. Then his father, too, disappeared (the Valhalla *motif* reveals to us, though not to Siegmund, that his father, 'Wolfe', was Wotan) and Siegmund, ill-starred always, was left to attain a hero's hardihood through the fighting of enemies and misfortune.

Birgit Nilsson as Brünnhilde

He now tells of the episode that has led to his present plight – an attempt to rescue a girl from a hated marriage forced on her by her relatives, which has ended only in the shattering of his spear and shield and flight through the forest. Cunningly, the Hunding *motif* shows us that it was his kinsmen who coerced the girl and fought Siegmund, and he has returned from a journey to avenge those whom Siegmund killed. Hunding in rage reveals the dramatic interweaving of their lives, but as host he cannot slay an unarmed guest. He brutally orders Sieglinde to prepare his drink for the night, and as she sets about it she shows her intuitive belief that Siegmund may be Wotan's predicted hero by constant glances at the sword in the ash-tree, which Siegmund, however, fails to understand.

But when the Hunding couple leave him, his reflections in the firelight centre, perhaps by telepathy, on the sword his father had promised him, and are intermingled with sweeter thoughts on the lovely woman who has just brought a first gentleness into his life. And for the first time he cries out to his father by his real name – Wälse – on a sustained high G flat, descending to its octave and followed by a similar octave-span on G natural, which (besides testing the breathing resources and vocal steadiness of the tenor) is a revealing climax of a soliloquy in song, "*Ein Schwert verhiess mir der Vater,*" penetrated almost throughout by the orchestra's reiteration of the Sword *motif*. But though the firelight catches the glint of the sword hilt (and in the music we hear the Sword *motif* flicker), Siegmund does not realise its significance.

Sieglinde, however, now joins him, having drugged Hunding's drink. Wagner's heroines are never lay figures, and Sieglinde no less than Isolde is ready, for all her gentleness, to take the initiative in a love affair. In her, too, flows the valiant blood of the unhappy Wälsungs, and she now tells Siegmund of the sword embedded in the tree by a stranger (Wotan) at her enforced wedding; of the softness of his glance at her, and his pronouncement that the weapon would belong only to the hero who had the power to withdraw it. This hero she feels sure is Siegmund, who brings love and consolation to her at last in her sufferings, and as the two ecstatically acknowledge their feelings, the door of the hut, in one of Wagner's moments of supreme magic, flies open, revealing the beauty of a spring night from which the tempest has departed. In the music we almost hear the glimmer of raindrops on the forest leaves, now bathed in moonlight: flutes and violins combine in trembling radiance as Siegmund in his Spring Song caresses and reassures the momentarily frightened Sieglinde. "*Keiner ging*" ("No one passed"), he sings – "*der Lenz lacht in den Saal*" (Spring spreads laughing over the earth). Winter storms have waned in the moonlight –

Sieglinde's response, *Du bist der Lenz* (Thou art the spring), is equally rapturous:

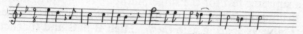

and its rippling orchestral undercurrent expresses her admission that, looking at herself in the stream, she has often seen *his* face, while her cry in the forest had echoed back to her in *his* voice. Memories stirring in her, she presses Siegmund to reveal his father's true name, Wälse – and the recognition of the twin brother and sister follows: a scene as radiant and moving in its mingling of joy with past pain as the recognition of Electra and Orestes from which Wagner doubtless drew some inspiration. Rising to a glorious high A, Sieglinde pronounces his name, Siegmund, and springing on to the table he grasps the sword and draws it from the tree.

Thus the sword which is to be handed down to Siegfried – *Nothung !* (Needful) – is named, brother and sister are reunited as bride and bridegroom, and with the sword for protection, heedless in their passion of Nemesis and tragedy, they rush into the forest.

The second act, "a wild and rocky pass", opens with music once again quick and ominous with storm, the Flight *motif* now associated with Siegmund and Sieglinde prominent with others such as the Sword and new Valkyrie themes in the texture:

Wotan in armour is directing Brünnhilde to give aid to Siegmund in his coming battle with Hunding, and we hear Brünnhilde's joyous, characteristic cry, "Ho-jo-to-ho!", with its high C's and B's and trilled ending: a strong adaptation of the agitated orchestral Valkyrie theme quoted above:

It is a supreme test for the singer, although it is worth noting here that Brünnhilde's top C's in the score are rare and Wagner was, in fact, always sparing with them. High B flats and (particularly) A's are, however, fairly plentiful in his soprano music, and Wotan's *tessitura*, with its prolonged high F's, is no less demanding in range – generating, in fact, t e hybrid "bass-baritone" voice, although Wagner himself once said (it is true, to lure a bass singer he wanted to sing the part) that he thought of Wotan as a true bass in vocal timbre.

The encounter and plans of father and daughter are quickly interrupted by Fricka, who now storms on to the scene as Brünnhilde leaves it. Hunding has appealed for aid from Valhalla against the fleeing foe who has stolen his wife, and easily won the outraged Fricka – goddess of chastity and marriage vows – to his side. Jealous, too, of Wotan's children, the Wälsungs, no less than of Brünnhilde, she engages him in a fierce battle of wills and argument and wins it in the face of his rage and scorching sorrow. For Wotan, caught in the web of his own laws, is blasted too by Fricka's scornful logic. The world can only be saved by man unaided by the Gods, that is Wotan's plan: yet Wotan has already helped Siegmund, the intended hero, by forging him the magic sword and planting it in the ash-tree. The great plan is already distorted: Siegmund, for morality's sake no less than Wotan's blunder, must be destroyed.

Fricka's inexorable, commanding notes are a feature of this scene, and her mezzo-soprano range as the aggrieved wife is given tis own winning melody:

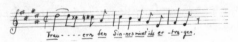

Trau - - - ern den Sin-nes müst'ich er -tra-gen.

90

Immune to such musical blandishments, Wotan's 'Anger' burns with dark frustration on the woodwind:

It is also known, often more aptly as regards feeling, as his 'Dejection' *motif*; and indeed it is more in sorrow than in anger that Wotan thinks throughout this scene, with a father's love and sense of betrayal, of the son Siegmund on whom he had set such hopes, yet whose tragic Wälsung destiny overrides his will. The *motif* is repeated over and over again in the orchestra as Fricka sings, together with those of the Wälsungs, and when she leaves, after wringing from Wotan a reluctant oath to withdraw his protection from Siegmund, Brünnhilde, bright for her errand, finds her father sunk in a disturbing misery. The Curse of the Ring has (the orchestra tells us) descended to his son; and throughout the following long duologue between father and daughter, in which Wotan narrates the story of the Ring and its evil power, we hear this poignant phrase of Dejection piercing the narrative with the other appropriate *motifs*.

Wotan tells us in addition something new: Fafner as a Dragon is guarding his precious Ring and treasure, but there is also a newcomer to the scene of whom we shall see much in *Götterdämmerung*. For Alberich, seducing a woman of the Gibichung race with gold, has begotten a son without love: the evil Hagen, who he hopes will win back the Ring. It is a darker parallel to Wotan's now dead hopes of Siegmund: and power, it seems, can still only be attained by the abnegation of love. The dark tones of the music anticipate Hagen's deep, ebony-bass when he grows to manhood in the later opera, and it is with bitterness and disillusion that Wotan bequeaths him the power and splendour he no longer himself values, and furiously (the more furious for his own inward pain) orders the protesting, distressed and loving Brünnhilde to transfer her protection to Hunding. There is guilt, too, behind his anger: for Brünnhilde is so close to him that she symbolises his conscience, and her rebellion is his own rebellion which he has, with such anguish, suppressed. Wagner's psychology in all such great conflicts of character (we have seen it in Lohengrin and Elsa, and will again in Tristan and Isolde) is absorbing and penetrating; and he understood more than most

Two British Siegmunds: Walter Hyde and....

dramatists the strange inter-
lockings of love and hate, of
conscience and defiance. And
a dreadful agony of soul, a
searing sorrow, pierces at such
times the rage and beauty of
his music.

Brünnhilde's final acqui-
escence is serener in its grief;
but she is heart-heavy as she
picks up her spear and passes
from view at the turbulent
approach of Siegmund and
Sieglinde. The lovers, in
flight, are in stormy and sorry
plight. Sieglinde – curiously
like Lady Macbeth – has
cracked under a strain her
earlier passion had not sus-
pected: her lyrical ecstasy now
alternates with a fever of guilt
and fear, and the tender,
strong Siegmund – quietly
sure himself in his love – can
do little to calm her. In her
frenzy she cries out for him
– "*Wo bist du, Siegmund?*" –
even when he is at her side,
and in a moment of clair-
voyance sees him perish with
broken sword while Wotan's
ash-tree, symbol of the Gods'
power, falls. When at last,
still hearing Hunding's horn
and hounds, she faints, Siegmund lays her head upon his
knees and watches over her
with a tender affection. It is
as if love and companionship
had at last brought him peace
and soothed his unhappiness

– his gentleness is a calm in stress born of resignation to ill-fate and suffering. This glows tranquilly but firmly through all the following scene – the wonderful *Todesverkündigung* scene with Brünnhilde in which it is the man who, with this spiritual integrity, overcomes the will of the goddess.

The scene opens with a Fate *motif* as mysterious in its way as that of the Tarnhelm:

It is repeated with varied modulations, and a muffled drumbeat punctuation that gives a strange effect of awe and is continued through much of the scene. Brünnhilde here, in fact, is a shadowy figure, a messenger of death: and Death follows Fate in a quiet but gravely noble theme:

Siegmund is mystically aware of his visitor – with his senses more than his eyes: and her opening cry is a command to

...Jon Vickers

him to look upon her:

At his awed query of her identity she has the deeply impressive reply: no one who looks on her face can escape his fate, which is death:

No one who has heard Kirsten Flagstad, greatest of modern Brünnhildes, in this scene will forget her bronze-like tones, the tones of a dark angel grave and inescapable. Lying largely in the

Kirsten Flagstad as Sieglinde...

mezzo or lower range of the voice, the music for this scene shows Wagner's wonderful instinct for musical drama and the nobility and awe of a fate directed by the Gods: Siegmund no less than Brünnhilde reflects it. She calls him to Valhalla and paints an heroic picture of the joys he will find there, including his father. But he can only think of the unconscious girl, the first to have shown him love and relieve his sorrow, and on learning Sieglinde cannot join him in Valhalla, but must live on earth to bear his son, he rejects Valhalla with violence and threatens to kill both Sieglinde and himself with Nothung – more especially as Brünnhilde has been forced to tell him that Wotan, who promised so much to the winner of the sword, has withdrawn his protection in the coming battle.

Brünnhilde, at first shocked, is ultimately moved by this un-yielding Wälsung quality of fighting destiny – and, too, by this strange revelation of the tender loyalty that can be aroused in a

...and as Brünnhilde

man by a woman he loves. We have seen and heard Brünnhilde as a loving daughter – but still the daughter of a God: now, in this scene in which she has appeared so imposingly as an immortal, remote and inhuman, we are conscious for the first time of the stirrings of womanhood which Siegfried, Siegmund's son, is later to bring to radiant flower. It is one of Wagner's most magical transformations: the music itself bounds into human passion as the two *hurl* notes and words at each other in a conflict that leaves the man the victor and the goddess, suddenly touched by human love and emotion, joyously aware again of her own and Wotan's deep inner desire to help Siegmund. She has made to Siegmund the promise that she will look after Sieglinde after his death: she now pledges herself to protect him in the coming fight. Her voice swings upwards, touching a winged and brilliant top A, before she departs with renewed confidence and happiness, even Wotan's wrath forgotten.

The thunderstorm that had accompanied Siegmund and Sieglinde's flight returns, and the stage darkens: yet the music softens to a piercing sweetness as Siegmund, tranquil again, bends over Sieglinde: we hear the echo of his Spring Song as well as the Death, Fate and (on muted cellos) Wälsung *motifs*. Hunding's horn intrudes, and while in the lightning flashes the foes search for each other, Sieglinde regains consciousness. In a dream she has relived the terror of her abduction from her burning home in childhood, and she is now only too distractedly aware of the coming danger to her lover. In the blackness Hunding's voice summons Siegmund (whom he still calls by the sad name the Wälsung had given himself, Wehwalt) to battle, and in the ensuing conflict on a craggy mountain ridge Brünnhilde is glimpsed hovering in protection. But Wotan, in rage, now appears and shatters Siegmund's sword with his spear, and in the opening of his foe's defences thus made Hunding lunges and kills instantly the unhappy warrior.

Brünnhilde, too aghast even to think of herself, seizes the now unconscious Sieglinde and the sword fragments and carries her away on her horse: and in the darkness we are aware of the dim but potently tragic figure of Wotan, gazing on the body of his slain son. For Hunding he has only contempt: go to Fricka, he commands icily, and tell her that Wotan's spear has avenged her sense of honour:

96

Amalie Materna: the first Brünnhilde at the Bayreuth Festival, 1876 →

The 'Go' is dangerously soft, almost weary, drained by sorrow for Siegmund, and at a slight contemptuous lift of Wotan's hand Hunding falls dead. Even as this happens we hear the Dejection *motif* gloomily descending in the orchestra: then rage succeeds numbness in the bereaved and disobeyed God, and murderously threatening revenge on Brünnhilde he stamps in terrible strides of wrath across the skyline, to music which reflects the tempest in his heart.

The third act.introduces us for the first time to Brünnhilde's eight sisters, the wild and lusty Valkyries, and the famous music depicting their ride with dead heroes on their saddles across the skies:

It has been fragmentarily heard in the opening to Act II. In the key of G minor and 9/8 rhythm, this music gives a tumultuous yet joyous grandeur to the scene, and it is hackneyed by use rather than its own nature. The Valkyries themselves, in shining armour and with welcoming lifts of their spears, arrive on the scene separately or in pairs: they are a jocular and happy group, not above humorous tauntings of each other. Wagner has blended the soprano and *mezzo* voices with skill, and fear pulses through them too when Brünnhilde arrives with her burden, Sieglinde, and tells them of her disobedience. Their terror of Wotan overwhelms any instinct to help her, and Sieglinde herself begs only to die. Only when Brünnhilde tells her of the coming Siegfried and gives her the shattered pieces of the sword Nothung does she rally: and we hear then a glorious musical phrase in which she expresses her joy and wonder at this miracle of motherhood that has befallen her, soaring to a high A in that lovely type of soprano *portamento* of which Wagner was a lyrical master:

It is the theme of Redemption by Love which will only appear again in the final Immolation scene of *Götterdämmerung*, riding noble and triumphant above the catastrophe of the Gods and the last dying tumult of the overflowing Rhine.

98

Friedrich Schorr as Wotan

Clutching the precious relics of the sword for her unborn son, Sieglinde disappears into the forest, while the cowering Valkyries await the storming approach of Wotan. "Where is Brünnhilde?" is his thundering cry, and the pleading of the sisters, hiding her in their midst, merely enflames his anger. Only Brünnhilde understood his will and spirit, he confesses: the betrayal and defiance hurt the deeper, and in the agony of that wound his Rage (the *motif* is hammered in the orchestra) burns without mercy. It draws Brünnhilde, humble and penitent, from the shelter of her sisters: she asks only for her sentence, which is a savage stripping from her of her rank as a Valkyrie, banishment from Valhalla, and a long sleep on this mountain peak from which the first man who finds her shall wake her, and claim her as his own.

The shrieks of the Valkyries proclaim the dreadful shame of this fate, and they are scattered quickly by a threat of Wotan's to bring on them a similar doom. Now only Brünnhilde remains to plead, and she does so, gently yet urgently, with a melting warmth that arouses something of Wotan's deep former affection. She knows her fate cannot be totally unsealed, Wotan's pride and decree as a God broken: she reminds him only that in protecting Siegmund she was obeying his own deepest unacknowledged wishes, and begs that at least she shall not fall to a dishonourable man, but be surrounded in her sleep by a fire which only the greatest hero can penetrate.

The first plea, though touching Wotan (who dare not face her) to the quick, arouses in him only a savage psychological reaction, born of his own pain: why should she give way to love while he, who loved Siegmund so deeply, must yield to the Curse and destroy him? His ironic taunting of her weakness is like the lash of a whip. Her attempt to cajole him with the story of the coming Siegfried has little more outward effect. But the accumulation of her agonised attempts to move him, and his own grief, forces him to grant her last request. Raising her from the ground and gazing at last into her eyes, his love returns full flood and it is with a deep and tender emotion that he takes his last farewell:

Its penetrating sorrow yields to a gentle Sleep *motif*:

as Wotan, to sweet *arpeggios*, guides Brünnhilde to a mound beneath a fir tree and lays her to rest; and then to a resurgence of Loge's fire music as the God summons him to strike the rock and encircle it with flames. In grandeur among the mounting fire music we hear the Siegfried *motif*, as Wotan declares that no one who fears his own spear shall break through the flames. It is his last cry in the opera, commanding in its rise to a splendid high E:

And in this grandeur of conflagration, lighting up the figure of the lonely God, and pierced softly by the *motif* of Fate, the opera majestically ends.

P. NADAR

Nadar

PARIS

Jean de Reszke as Siegfried

Siegfried

Siegfried has been called the *scherzo* of *The Ring*, and it is indeed Wagner's 'happy' opera, as Shaw noted. Yet its Prelude suggests forest gloom, with a brooding *motif*:

which is associated both with Mime and the dragon, Fafner, sleepily guarding his treasure. Both are enemies of the boy Siegfried, whose bright dawn of life and rustic innocence form the *scherzo* and humour of the story.

Sieglinde had died in giving birth to her son, and by evil chance had been tended in her last moments by Alberich's brother, the dwarf Mime, who has brought up the boy in his cave in the forest, and treasured the splinters of the magic sword, in the hope of using the boy to kill Fafner and seize the Ring for himself. For the boy he has no glimmer of affection; in his greed for the gold, like Alberich, he has foresworn love. The two are of a different kind and metal, and even the boy can see through the dwarf's attempts to gain his trust and unbelievable declaration that they are father and son. For Siegfried is a child of Nature, who, reflecting on his solitary life in the forest, has watched the birds and animals and noted their mating, and the bringing forth of young in the image of themselves.

We are to hear his impatient questioning of Mime on these things very soon in the opera, but at first Mime is alone in his smithy, ill-humouredly trying after many failures to re-forge the fragments of the sword. The hammering Nibelungen *motif* punctuates his efforts. But Siegfried enters and brightness with him: brightness in the ringing sound of his silver hunting horn:

and equally vivacious *motif* of exuberance, full of energy and hurry:

103

The horn *motif* is a call we are to hear many times in *Siegfried*, and with an added maturity and heroic grandeur (with a change of key and tempo) in *Götterdämmerung*, where it also forms a part of the Funeral March:

He is the young hero free from guile, beloved of Wagner as a Redeemer, and developed spiritually and mystically in *Parsifal* later. Shaw has finely characterised him:

"The boy Siegfried, having no god to instruct him in the art of unhappiness, inherits none of his father's (i.e. Siegmund's) ill-luck, and all his father's hardihood. The fear against which Siegmund set his face like flint, and the woe which he wore down, are unknown to the son... He is enormously strong, full of life and fun, dangerous and destructive to what he dislikes, and affectionate to what he likes; so that it is fortunate that his likes and dislikes are sane and healthy. Altogether an inspiriting young forester, a son of the morning, in whom the heroic race has come out into the sunshine from the clouds of his grandfather's majestic entanglements with law, and the night of his father's tragic struggle with it."

Lauritz Melchior as Siegfried

His first action after frightening Mime with a bear he has captured in the forest is to snap on the anvil the sword the dwarf has managed to forge. Mime's whining recitation (which he has heard too often) of his kindness in rearing him meets only with his contempt. He cannot understand why, hating the dwarf so much, he must always return to him. Mime insinuatingly tries to suggest that love brings him back, and is met with the boy's experiences, already mentioned, among the animals in the forest. There is loneliness in the boy's reflections: where is Mime's mate, where his own? Who were his father and mother? The orchestra weaves the Wälsung *motif* which he cannot understand, but his own yearning for love is expressed with mellifluous charm.

Mime's obvious lies madden him, and clutching him by the throat he suddenly has an instinct of the secret that binds him to the dwarf: the identity of his parents. Mime at last is forced to reveal the truth, and tells him of Sieglinde and Nothung, the shattered sword of his father. Sieglinde's music gives a poignancy to the scene, and Siegfried, thinking of her death, has a stab of pathos. "*So starb meine Mutter an mir?*": the phrase is low, ruminative:

So starb mei-ne Mut-ter an mir?

It is a sensitive moment for the tenor, this musing pang of realisation that he caused his mother's death: and he is later to wonder innocently if all mothers must die at their children's birth. There is much potential depth of affection in the young Siegfried; but now he rallies with the buoyancy of youth and, happy that at least Mime is not his father, departs for his beloved woods with a command that the dwarf must try again to weld together Siegmund's broken sword.

As Mime broods disgustedly on this unlikely achievement, a nobler theme is heard in the music, the *motif* of Wotan the Wanderer who now journeys across the earth, watching events and haunted by his sense of the coming fall of the Gods. The broad, expansive, majestic chords:

paint him as a tragic figure, with some affinities indeed to the wandering Flying Dutchman of Wagner's earlier opera. He has

105

Set Svanholm as Siegfried

aged, and carries a traveller's staff; yet, as we are to see, his new and saddened philosophy is pierced by an occasional wry humour. He by no means pacifies the frightened dwarf by proposing Mime should set him three questions, which will lose him his head should he fail to answer them. Mime, losing his own head in another sense, asks him three easy questions – the names of the races that dwell below, on and above the surface of the earth (appropriate *motifs*). But Wotan's description of Valhalla and of his spear, the symbol of power, in answer to the third question, carry terror with them: he touches the earth with the spear and thunder petrifies the dwarf. Wotan now proposes three riddles of his own: the identity of the race whom Wotan, loving them, yet ruined; the name of the sword with which Siegfried will slay Fafner; and who will forge the sword? Mime answers the first two easily enough, encouraged by the stranger's genial laughter, and oblivious to the irony beneath it. But the last he cannot answer, and Wotan prompts him: he who is without fear will forge Nothung anew. Leaving Mime's forfeited head for Siegfried to deal with, Wotan departs, amused yet still strangely god-like: we hear the Fire Music as he disappears into the forest, herald of Siegfried's destiny and success.

A mass of *motifs* now play around the terrified dwarf, as weird lights from the forest play around his head. Trembling with superstition he is found by Siegfried, who immediately demands his sword. Mime to test him tries to teach him the meaning of fear, and the Fire *motif* suggests that Siegfried will learn this only from Brünnhilde. The shuddering music paints this fear as vividly as Mime's words, but Siegfried is uncomprehending – even guileless enough to wish he possessed this bewitching accomplishment. In such subtle touches Wagner draws the portrait of this uncorrupted youth, whose simplicity matches Parsifal's own. But it is obvious the dwarf cannot forge the sword, and now Siegfried sets to at the anvil and furnace himself, while Mime excitedly prepares a poisonous brew with which to slay him should he prove successful and dispose of the Dragon.

Meanwhile, the lusty hero sings a Smelting Song based on his father's cry of 'Nothung' which we have heard at the end of *Die Walküre*, and follows it, as his work triumphantly progresses, with the Forging Song:

This unremitting labour and lung power are rewarded: the sword is successfully welded, and Siegfried cleaves through the anvil at one blow, as the orchestra soars into a joyous outburst.

At the opening of the second act Wagner's wizardry carries us mysteriously into the sombre darkness of the forest, where Fafner is guarding his treasure. We hear his heart-beats through his *motif* as he slumbers:

And because Alberich is there, glooming about his lost treasure in front of Fafner's cave, we hear, too, the Ring *motif*. A flicker of wind and light accompanies Wotan, who now confronts the dwarf. As Alberich, unlike Mime, has any amount of gumption, this encounter is considerably more dramatic than the over-long and rather unnecessary 'riddle' scene of the previous act. He hurls defiance and hatred at Wotan with all the vehemence of which his character and Wagner's dramatic musicianship are capable, but the God, calm in his fatalism, is unruffled in dignity and denies all personal interest in acquiring the gold. But he warns Alberich that the Ring in fact is destined to be won by another, and of his brother Mime's schemes. And his own voice deepens in sorrow – perhaps with memory of the dead Siegmund, perhaps prophetic of his own doom – as he names Siegfried as the only possible redeemer of Alberich's Curse on the Ring. Otherwise the inheritance belongs to Alberich's own son, Hagen.

Before he goes Wotan calls on Fafner to warn him of his coming foe, but the Giant is sleepily indifferent:

He is in possession – let him slumber. And Wotan laughs ironically as he tells Alberich (Erda *motif*) that destiny is in any case settled. Once again warning him of his brother, he takes his departure, the wind in the forest tossing the Sword, Valkyrie Ride, Wotan's Farewell and other *motifs* about the orchestra like autumn leaves.

108

Now there are only Fafner's heart-beats as Alberich slips out of view: and with the coming of the dawn we hear Siegfried and Mime approaching, bringing new and exuberant life. With Fafner's lair at hand, the dwarf again tries in vain to teach the young hero the meaning of fear, and in the end, considering discretion the better part of valour, he departs to a nearby spring to await the result of the coming conflict. The richening web of *motifs* and their variations as the *Ring* cycle progresses is never more apparent, and the *Siegfried* score shows a marvellous inventiveness and dramatic aptness in its orchestral texture. But there is now a lull as Siegfried lies down to rest under a lime tree (that tree under which Wagner left him for so many years) and the rustling of leaves brings a new theme deliciously redolent of the stirrings of life and breeze in a summer wood – the Forest Murmurs:

Against these rippling semi-quavers in E major Siegfried's thoughts wander on the meaning of life and on his parents: Wälsung, Flight and the Sieglinde Love themes glimmer, as it were, among the trees. He wonders if all mothers die in giving birth, and if the language of the birds overhead could tell him more of Sieglinde. These magical bird notes flutter on woodwind through the scene (Wagner was inspired by many of their variations during his walks in the Sihl Valley), and Siegfried tries to imitate them on a cut reed and his horn – with some unfortunate results in pitch:

But at least the efforts awaken Fafner, who yawningly advances to his doom on Siegfried's sword. Before he expires, in a theatrically satisfying bellow of smoke, the Giant warns Siegfried of Mime's purpose: and Siegfried, hastily putting his hand hot with dragon's blood to his lips, finds he can suddenly understand the song of the birds. One tells him of the Tarnhelm and Ring in the cave, and as he goes to seek them Mime tremulously returns, only to launch into a bitter scene of recrimination with Alberich, to music of jerky, quarrelsome rhythm. As they withdraw, spitting hatred in sound, Siegfried emerges from the cave. He has both Tarnhelm and Ring but, uncorrupted, has no suspicion of their

109

Siegfried confronts Fafner, Bayreuth 1952

power, and the gold he has left untouched. The Ring, a pretty trinket, he places on his finger. The woodbird warns him, however, of Mime's treachery and as a result, when he returns, Siegfried is able correctly to interpret the caressing phrases with which the dwarf fondly imagines he is addressing him (this combination of tender, insinuating music with virulent words is achieved by Wagner with much skill, the grovelling flourish of Mime's bows to the boy being amusingly depicted in music). Sickened, Siegfried kills Mime with one stroke of Nothung and lays his body with that of the Dragon. And now a new joy awaits him, for the bird sings gaily of the sleeping Brünnhilde whom only a hero, who can penetrate the guarding flames, can awaken. It is with the enraptured promise of a mate and companion of his own kind that the youth follows the flight of the bird.

The third act opens in the lonely place at the foot of the rocks where Brünnhilde lies. Wotan, near his end, has come to consult Erda; and we hear his Nemesis, the Treaty *motif*, in many variations as well as the mysterious effect of Erda's rising from the depths in response to Wotan's command. But her warnings are now superfluous, however noble in musical substance, for the God already knows his fate. To Siegfried falls the Heritage of the World:

Traditional setting for Act II, Covent Garden. Set Svanholm as Siegfried

And as the splendid new *motif* rings out Erda sinks back into her earthly sleep and we await the coming of the hero who will learn wisdom and fear from Wotan's daughter, and guidance from her love.

The scene between Wotan and his grandson is the last in which we shall see the doomed God: and it is psychologically one of Wagner's most revealing creations. Siegfried, unconscious of course of the Wanderer's identity, is soon impatient of the conversation and spear barring his way, and angrily shatters the weapon with his sword; but it is Wotan's tragedy that the scene underlines. The whole episode is a revelation of human character – the grandfather's (as well as Creator's) pride and affection, a little amused at the boy's importunity and disrespect, finally angry at it; jealous, too, in a sudden pang, of Brünnhilde, the child who represents his 'real' self and inner conscience, as well as of his loss of authority. The Wotan who picks up his broken spear is a destroyed and superseded, and therefore tragic, human being, as well as an instrument of law and authority laid low. As so often with Wagner, the *symbol* of power is given imaginative force through human character and emotion. When a great artist, such as the modern Wotan, Hans Hotter, stoops and picks up the shattered spear, and slowly retreats into the shadows, we are

111

Siegfried' Act III, Bayreuth production by Wieland Wagner

conscious of Wagner's genius in the transformation of the myth
into music-drama: the more so when, as in this case, the actor-
singer has earlier shown us a Wotan of supreme majesty, torn by
anger and also all the subtleties of human grief.

The way to the summit is now free to Siegfried, who to the
radiantly leaping Fire Music plunges through the flames and emerges on the rocky heights. The scene is that of Act III of *Die Walküre*, where Brünnhilde, shield on breast and spear at her side, lies
like the sleeping beauty of the fairy tale. As the flames die down
we are conscious of the blueness of the sky, and a luminous
sweetness of melodic line given to the violins accompanies Siegfried's appearance. The *motifs*, including the basic Rhinegold
theme, are like an exquisitely fine mesh of sound as the boy,
wondering at this apparent warrior, gently removes 'his' helmet
and is startled by the flowing hair. Wonder changes to shock as he
removes the shield; and it is to a sudden violent burst of music
that he starts back and cries "*Das ist kein Mann!*" The naivety is
one of Wagner's characteristic touches of humour; and indeed
perhaps only Wagner could have dared and got away with the
half-amusing, half-touching situation early in the love duet which
follows, when Siegfried, misled by a phrase of Brünnhilde's and
confusing the nature of womanhood and the love he feels beating
within him, guilelessly assumes that his mother, after all, did not
die and Brünnhilde must be Sieglinde! Brünnhilde's gentle cor-
rection is a model of tenderness and tact.

But at first Siegfried's lovely discovery is not easy to wake: as again in the fairy tale, only the happy thought of a kiss induces her to open her eyes. And her first response is not to Siegfried but to the sunlight, to which she lifts her frozen arms in the returning joy of life:

She has woken to ravishing harp *arpeggios*, following a lift of the music like a burst of sunshine and interspersed with silvery soaring phrases on the violins:

and although she is glad to learn her deliverer is Siegfried, and tells him of her pity for the Wälsungs, she is by no means ready at once to forget her godhead and yield to womanhood. Her fear inspires Siegfried to repeat his cries, '*Erwaken!*' with which he had tried to awaken her from a more literal sleep, and eventually, indeed, his ardour awakes in her a new feminine passion and joy. The love duet, radiantly challenging the future, yet full of musical echoes of the past, weaves its new themes in a rapturous texture. Siegfried's Hail to Love:

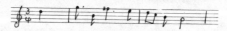

which Brünnhilde echoes, urges the conflicting emotions forward into an Enthusiasm for Love:

which is like the chiming of wedding bells; but tenderness, too, intervenes in the tranquil Peace theme in E major heard only in this duet:

113

It is sweetly introduced on the strings and taken up by Brünnhilde until the gentle music excitens and bears her on its wings to an ecstatic top C. The *finale* is a counterpoint and harmony of voices, characteristically in this happy opera joining the lovers in fragments of laughter:

And on Brünnhilde's radiant and laughing high C, with Siegfried completing the octave chord, the curtain begins to fall. But ominously, the last word is '*Tod*': the lovers are laughing, as they admit, at Death.

'Siegfried': Hermann Uhde as the Wanderer (Wotan), Bayreuth, 1960

Götterdämmerung

Götterdämmerung – the Twilight of the Gods – opens with a Prologue in two scenes: the first in which the three Norns or Fates (Urd, Verdandi and Skuld in northern mythology, though perhaps with purpose Wagner impersonalises them into first, second and third Norn) recount the tragedy of the Gods and complete their task as the rope of fate they are weaving breaks; the second showing Brünnhilde and Siegfried parting in the dawn after their union.

The opening chords are those of Brünnhilde's Hail to the Sun on awakening from her sleep, but the undulations of the Rhine flow from them, and we hear, too, softly, the sombre theme of Fate which has been so potent a thread in the fabric of the *Todesverkündigung* scene in *Die Walküre*. The orchestral prelude is, however, brief and the Norns in turn recount how Wotan visited the spring at the root of the world ash-tree, and sacrificed an eye in exchange for the wisdom a drink from the spring brought him; how his spear, made from a branch of the tree and inscribed with the 'runes' of wisdom (the source of his power) was shattered by the hero Siegfried; and how the Gods now await their downfall, in a Valhalla surrounded by faggots made of the world ash-tree which Wotan has felled. The Norns are ageing and have difficulty in fastening their rope, now worn by the edge of the rock. They recall at the last Alberich's stealing of the gold, and his Curse of the Ring. As the third Norn pulls the rope it breaks: their prophecy and wisdom are at an end, and they sink into the earth, finally at rest.

In spite of the many familiar *motifs* woven into this scene of recapitulation, with its warning of the end of Valhalla and the Gods, it has a musical quality of its own, mysterious and fateful: and in fact it is a characteristic of *Götterdämmerung*, now the heroic cycle draws to its close, that the splendid musical score retains its individuality while weaving the many *motifs* already known into the fabric in new and dramatic combinations and modulations. Inevitably, there are fewer new *motifs* now, but new melody is still abundant: the Norns have their share of it, with a strangely sombre link between their several narratives, as they pass on rope and story to each other:

115

The Fate theme (*ppp*) and Loge's flames echo faintly as the Norns vanish, and as night is slowly transformed into daybreak, the music, '*molto tranquillo*', peacefully expands. The sweet theme of Brünnhilde, the woman, is heard first on the woodwind:

and later triumphantly in the full orchestra, as she and Siegfried appear from their cave in the brightening light of the morning sun. His Call of the Woods, too, rings out in a transformed splendour:

and as Brünnhilde opens their duet, which so miraculously engenders new beauties without repeating the *Siegfried* duet heard so recently, her womanhood theme flows softly beneath her opening words. She has taught Siegfried her Goddess' wisdom, and now with Gräne, her beloved horse, and the sword Nothung, sends him into the world to complete his mission.

Tenderness and joy alternate in the lovers' music, a beautiful theme on the strings following her declaration of faith in his undying love:

Their parting is ecstatic and untroubled, a paean of joy ending in one of her rare and radiant high C's, and as she waves to him he descends into the valley of the Rhine, his passage marked by the famous music often played in the concert hall as "Siegfried's Journey to the Rhine". We hear the gay, valiant call of his horn and the surge and murmur of the Rhine waters in flowing measures:

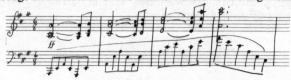

And at the end the soft chords of the Rhinemaidens' cry of 'Rheingold' remind us of the stolen gold, forever at the back of the Nemesis of this opera.

The scene changes now to the first act proper: a scene new to us, the Hall of the great human race of the Gibichungs. Its massive pillars only partially mask a background open to the Rhine, and almost immediately the music gives us a sombre sign of the evil Hagen (son of Alberich and half-brother to the young Gibichungs, Gunther and Gutrune) whose dark personality is to work tragic havoc in this opera:

The aspiring, rather syncopated *motif* of the ambitious Gibichungs quickly follows, and is heard frequently beneath the conversation of Hagen and Gunther:

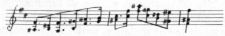

Hagen, his own sinister ends fixed on the acquisition of the Ring, is tortuously scheming, and for his purposes he plays on the Gibichung pride of race by drawing Gunther's and Gutrune's attention to their need to marry. To Gunther he pictures the sleeping Brünnhilde, a noble bride, who however can only be reached by Siegfried, the foretold hero who is destined to penetrate the flames that guard her. If Siegfried can be persuaded to win her for Gunther, the hero himself may wed the gentle Gutrune. And he tells just enough of the story of the Ring and the treasure to add the dazzle of power-temptation to the match: concealing, of course, the fact that Siegfried has already rescued Brünnhilde and is wedded to her. Gutrune is the prize for which Siegfried will win Brünnhilde for Gunther; and the Tarnhelm will enable him to take Gunther's form in doing it, and deceive Brünnhilde as to her rescuer.

The success of this plan depends on the psychology of Gunther and Gutrune, and it is on this that Hagen shrewdly hazards all. Both are weak and easily led, and although Gunther has some flashes of hurt pride they are quickly stilled by his inflamed passion for Brünnhilde and sense of family greatness in store. Gutrune's humility cannot imagine so great a hero as Siegfried loving her; but the shining vision excites the young girl enough for her to agree to Hagen's solution – a potion bringing total forgetfulness of past affection and transferring it to the woman who hands him the draught. It is true she has no knowledge of any previous woman in Siegfried's life and enters the plot with no conception of its bringing any real harm to Siegfried or anyone else. Her faith in her own charm is too weak for her to question the need for the draught. There is something touching and artless in Gutrune that wins her our sympathy: ready in affection, modest and loyal, she is the unsuspecting victim of the policy and greed of others.

Her *motif* is a sweet and docile one, like herself:

We are to hear it in seductive beauty soon beneath her words of welcome, when Siegfried, having drunk the potion, first gazes on her. Hagen's tale, of course, is a mass of familiar musical echoes from the past, and as his scheme succeeds with his hearers Siegfried's horn sounds in the distance, with its characteristic call and Rhine music in the orchestra. Hagen watches the progress of his boat upstream and himself offers to tether his horse when he lands. Gutrune, gazing in wonder and expectation on the fabulous hero, withdraws to fetch the treacherous drink of hospitality at Hagen's gesture (its mysterious *motif* is based on that of the Tarnhelm, which we are to hear much in this act).

Siegfried has heard of the fame of the Gibichungs, and unsuspectingly seeks their hospitality and friendship in his travels. Gunther welcomes him with some genuine show of good feeling, but when Hagen returns he questions him closely about the treasure he acquired by the slaying of the dragon. Siegfried is as artless and careless about it as is his wont: he shows the Tarnhelm, and describes the Ring he has left as a pledge of love with "the noblest of women" (Gunther, of course, does not realise this is Brünnhilde). The treasure he has left in the dragon's cave. It is Hagen who enlightens him as to the magic power of the Tarnhelm, but Siegfried's interest is dispelled by the entry of Gutrune with the drink.

This is a key moment in the drama, betraying Siegfried into a treachery and disloyalty not in his own nature. It is a pity Wagner had to resort to it, for he rarely uses magic except as a means of bringing true psychological forces to the surface (the first act of

118

Tristan is a notable example). It adds the tortuousness of mistaken identity to the plot of *The Ring*, and in a sense complicates and falsifies its motivation and climax. Siegmund, wronged by Fate, had still a hand – through his fatal love for Sieglinde – in his own tragic destiny. Siegfried, his son and the intended greater hero, can only fall victim to an inhuman contrivance – operated by another's lust for power, yet still not touching any facet of his own psychology. His innocence keeps for us some of his essential integrity to the end: in all outside the potency of the draught he is Siegfried, joyous, strong, courageous and loving, still. In all actions driven by it he is a mechanism without soul, and loses as a vital force in the final catastrophe as a result.

In spite of the moving redemption of his death, a mortal truly betrayed and heroic in his great musical farewell, he is no longer in this opera the real hero of the tragedy. These are Brünnhilde, the betrayed, and the invisible Wotan, the immortal power destroyed. They are great enough, opposed by the Satanic personality of Hagen, to carry the work dramatically to its tremendous conclusion. But only the musical-dramatic genius of Wagner hides to some extent the mechanical contrivance and Siegfried's loss of stature. The opera in adequate performance has the theatrical power of Greek tragedy; but even the fated heroes of Greek drama contributed to Nemesis through their own character or *hubris*, and Siegfried is no Oedipus plunging voluntarily into disaster, blinded by his own intemperate search for truth and inflammable tyranny when thwarted.

His fall nevertheless has pathos, and his natural fidelity is revealed in his thoughts of Brünnhilde even as he drinks the fatal draught (we hear a fragment of the love duet as he drinks). His awakening to Gutrune's charm is at once obvious; he asks Gunther her name, and by some telepathic instinct immediately asks if Gunther himself has a wife. The story of Gunther's desire for Brünnhilde, and need for help, is soon divulged; for an instant or two, while Loge's flames flicker in the orchestra, Siegfried struggles with a last stirring of memory, but Brünnhilde's name means nothing to him, and the mysterious Tarnhelm *motif* prompts his generously-meant offer to penetrate the fire and, disguised by the Tarnhelm as Gunther, win his new friend a bride.

The poignant pang of half-memory (which only a highly intelligent actor of Siegfried, like the Swedish Set Svanholm, will fully reveal) is past: he is gay and energetic, and eagerly welcomes

'Götterdämmerung' Act II: Bayreuth production by Wieland Wagner

Gunther's suggestion of an oath of blood-brotherhood. Pricking their arms, and drinking Hagen's fresh wine, they make a solemn vow of friendship, Gunther's baritone finely phrasing a solemn yet stirring theme:

Bru-der brün-stig mu- thig ge- mischt blüh' im Trank un-ser Blut!

The voices, tenor and baritone, echo and harmonise in passionate spiritual union: but in the orchestra there are ominous references to Wotan's fatal Treaty and Alberich's Curse of the gold. And when Siegfried turns to ask why Hagen has not joined in the bond, Alberich's son darkly indicates his own blood is not noble enough. We get a stark, brief glimpse of the Nibelung and the writhing, if subconscious, inferiority complex fomenting beneath Hagen's hatred and intent to destroy both Gunther and Siegfried; and when the two depart on their quest (the Fire Music and Siegfried's Rhine Journey themes sparkle in the orchestra), he sits guarding the Hall in a menacing stillness, morosely brooding on his plan to orchestral repetitions of the '*Rheingold*' cry. These continue in the texture of the music that follows, leading us back to Brünnhilde happily con-

'Götterdämmerung' Act II: Covent Garden 1954 (L. to R.) Dezsö Ernster as Hagen, Margaret Harshaw as Brünnhilde, Hermann Uhde as Gunther

templating her Ring and recalling, without regret, her Valkyrie past. Thunder resounds among the mountains, and fragments of the Ride herald the approach of Waltraute.

Brünnhilde's sister has come to her in a last desperate attempt to forestall the end of the Gods, to which Wotan their father is resigned. Brünnhilde welcomes her gladly, and is moved as we are by her poignant picture of the scene at Valhalla, to which Wotan has returned with his spear in splinters. There he now sits in dejection, surrounded by the heroes he has summoned and with funeral pyre ready, and not all Waltraute's love and tenderness can move him, only the thought of Brünnhilde whom he still loves.

Waltraute's narration is long and musically deeply affecting, sombrely cast for a mezzo-soprano voice and lovely in its soft and dreamy passages, while the orchestra is hushed to a gentle drumbeat. But when Waltraute explains her true mission – to beg Brünnhilde to return the Ring to the Rhinemaidens and stay the Curse that will ruin them all – her sister's womanhood asserts itself immediately over her revived feelings as a Valkyrie, and her love and pity for Wotan himself. The Ring given her by Siegfried shall never leave her finger, and Waltraute is forced to depart with fatalistic cries of despair.

Thus the Fate of the Gods is sealed by Brünnhilde herself, and with appalling irony retribution now comes upon her. For Siegfried approaches through the flames, and although at first she joyously prepares to welcome him she is soon aware that the mysterious figure that appears, his face half-masked by the Tarnhelm, is not her lover. The figure is ominous, black against the skyline, and Fate and the Gibichung themes conflict with others in the music. Siegfried seems transformed in character no less than body; when she claims the Ring will protect her, he brutally wrenches it from her finger. Her passion and her hope are spent, and her only comment now is the dazed, broken:

And as she staggers to the cave, he draws his sword which he swears shall be placed between them to protect Gunther's honour. Ironically, we hear her theme of womanhood, and the sharp, explosive chords of the Siegfried-Gunther blood-bond that characterise the scene:

The Prelude to the second act is dominated by the sombreness associated with Hagen, still waiting by the Hall of the Gibichungs, but now on the river side. The Rhinegold cry permeates the music, and in the darkness of night we dimly become aware of the figure of Alberich beside his sleeping son:

Alberich's insinuating, whispered phrase recurs in the scene, superbly pointing its brooding, trance-like atmosphere. For Hagen's responses are indeed those of one in a trance, as Alberich, to the accompaniment of the Nibelung hate *motif* and a new one of Murder, recounts in gloating triumph Wotan's waiting at Valhalla and coming downfall, and urges his son to destroy Siegfried, inheritor of the Ring and treasure, and win them back for their own power.

At last he goes, satisfied his son will avenge the stealing of the gold; and Hagen ominously waits on as the dawn breaks, and Siegfried's joyous horn call heralds his approach. He has, he recounts, won Brünnhilde and she and Gunther are following him; but his first desire now is for Gutrune. Hagen, in a sinister 'Hoi-ho' we are to come to know only too well, calls for her. Siegfried's thoughts are only of marrying her, but he again recounts his tale, at which she wonders and also expresses fear of him (it is a neat psychological touch, this blend of hero-worship and timidity in Gutrune). They depart to prepare for a double wedding, and Hagen, alone, mounts a high rock and summons the Gibichung vassals with his mighty, menacing call:

He uses a cow-horn, and continues summoning them to arm for strife until they appear in clusters on the rocks, bringing to the *Ring* cycle its first full male chorus in grand opera tradition. They are a rough but not ungenial band, and the false geniality Hagen himself assumes with them only adds to the sinister menace we feel in his character. He assures them they are needed only for a wedding, and to give ritualistic offerings to Wotan and the Gods. His darker purpose in summoning them armed they do not discern. And so in the lusty choral harmonies we are conscious continually of the Marriage Call:

Gunther and Brünnhilde now enter from their boat, and the Vassals welcome them enthusiastically, while Gunther (preceded by a fragment of the Valkyrie Ride) presents his bride proudly as the noblest of women. Brünnhilde herself is pale and silent; but when Gunther greets the approaching Siegfried and Gutrune, coupling their names, she looks up and gazes on Siegfried with incredulity. In the succeeding hush (the Tarnhelm *motif* faintly sounds) everyone notes her distress, and wonders at it; and the more so when in reply to Siegfried's unbelievable statement that he is to marry Gutrune, as she Gunther, she rouses herself to a vehement denial. The effort is too much for her, weakened already by uncomprehending suffering, and as she collapses in Siegfried's arms she is capable only of a broken, piteous:

But indeed he knows her not, and is only puzzled by her behaviour.

Then she sees the Ring on his finger, and fury begins to replace despair. She accuses Gunther angrily of giving Siegfried the Ring he snatched from her, and, when he denies it, is only enraged further by Siegfried's equal denial and statement (for the Tarnhelm theme warns us he has forgotten even the details of his recent encounter with her) that he won it by destroying the dragon. Now Hagen insinuates a suggestion to the Vassals that Siegfried has gained the Ring by some trickery, and Brünnhilde in the stress of her agony blazes out a similar accusation of deceit, followed by a bitter cry to the Gods at their apparent betrayal of her. It is Siegfried, not Gunther, who is her husband, she storms, and this indeed creates a stir, for it suggests Siegfried has betrayed Gunther while actually winning his bride. Siegfried (Wagner is very inconsistent in the memories he allows him) passionately denies it, and to the Blood-Brotherhood *motif* swears the sword Nothung lay between him and Brünnhilde that night; and reinforces his oath on Hagen's spear. Ironically (for Hagen's spear is indeed to kill him) he declares, let this steel pierce him if he truly betrayed Gunther.

Brünnhilde by now has flamed into a different kind of woman from the one we have known. Her tenderness betrayed by events, the Valkyrie in her aroused to a God-like fury of vengeance, she tears Siegfried's hand from the spear and, placing her own upon it, vows in ice-riven phrases that she is speaking the truth:

In respect of the past, of course, she is doing so – and has no knowledge of the terrible blank in Siegfried's memory. This prompts her one deliberate lie – that he also betrayed Gunther (for she grasps now that it was not Gunther who penetrated the flames) in the cave. In her own mind it is all one – Siegfried's treachery to *her* is incontestable and despicable, and in her anguish and disillusion revenge is the only thing her distraught mind can grasp at with any relief. Siegfried, merely bewildered and innocent enough with regard to the emotions of women, takes it all with a not unlikeable display of good-humour, and tries to raise Gunther's spirits by suggesting that all this is only woman's hurt pride – the Tarnhelm disguise was obviously insufficient and Brünnhilde is shocked and mortified at the trick played on her. With this he sweeps Gutrune off the stage, together with the Vassals who are reassured by his untroubled sincerity. The Wedding Call, Curse and Rhinegold themes all penetrate the silence after their turbulent departure. Only Brünnhilde, Gunther and Hagen now remain.

Brünnhilde's fire is spent, her bitterness wearily intoned:

The whole poignant irony of her position is in that low, despairing line: of what use, indeed, is her goddess' wisdom when confronted with the problems of human passion and treachery? Betrayed by Gods and men, she stands helpless in an alien world.

Gunther, a lonely, weak man, who seems to have valued Siegfried's friendship, is plunged in equal gloom. But Hagen, always morose, is alert to foment trouble. He offers to avenge Brünnhilde, and conceals the lash to his proud nature of her contempt: how can *he* overcome Siegfried, still to her – in spite of her pain – a glorious hero? He then presses from her the secret of Siegfried's one weakness. Her goddess' wisdom had made him invulnerable; but his back was unprotected, for Siegfried, who knows not fear, would never flee from his enemies. There, swears Hagen immediately, he will strike him; and as he rouses the shamed and unhappy Gunther to the murder we hear the ominous phrase of Siegfried's Death:

Gunther, more appalled than in agreement, echoes the cry, and he is torn by the memory of his oath of brotherhood as well as thoughts of his sister's distress. Hagen, however, brushes this aside: they will take Siegfried hunting and pretend he has been slain by a boar. Brünnhilde, an unyielding, avenging heroine of Greek tragedy now, adds her urging of Siegfried's death, and the unhappy man, trapped between these two stronger personalities, finally assents. The trio which follows cements the vow in a splendidly dramatic flare of operatic vocal writing: Murder and Conspiracy *motifs* ominously underline Siegfried's doom, and Hagen in the bass stave dreams greedily of the Ring and the power which it will bring him. And by one of Wagner's striking conflicts of mood the Marriage Call breaks in joyously on the trio, as the Vassals enter carrying the unsuspecting Siegfried and Gutrune aloft on their shields. Into this bridal procession Brünnhilde is reluctantly drawn by Gunther as the curtain falls.

Siegfried's horn call off-stage opens the third act. He is out on the fatal chase, and the scene is now the banks of the Rhine. Once again we hear the mounting cadences of its waves, and the Rhine-maidens splashing in its waters and venturing out into the sunlight at the foot of the cliffs. It is a scene of youth and freshness, a pleasant diversion after the vengeance-ridden drama of the preceding act. Siegfried, who is ahead of the others in the hunt, soon joins the singing maidens and takes some delight in them. But when they beg his Ring of him he refuses to part with it, for Gutrune's sake, and resists their taunts of his subservience to his wife. Yet as the charming girls swim away he has a moment of shame and compunction at his apparent meanness, and offers them the Ring. But their mood, too, has changed: they warn him of the Curse on it, and at this he replaces it calmly on his finger. Siegfried's very lack of fear is to be an element in his own doom. The Rhinemaidens leave him: the brief lyrical interlude is over. The Curse invades the music, and with it the sound of the approaching hunting horns and Hagen's sinister 'Hoi-ho!'

Siegfried greets his friends with a ringing echo of Hagen's cry, rising to a joyous top C. As the company settle down to a picnic meal, he explains with his usual tranquillity that the Rhinemaidens have just foretold his coming death. There is something touching in Siegfried's extrovert personality, the artless naivety of his courage which has not the imagination to fear death, or suspect the treachery of others. Gunther, the introvert, starts at his remark, and his unhappiness is so apparent that Siegfried presses a drink on him, and urges him not to worry about Brünnhilde's moods. His trustful good humour only sharpens Gunther's pang of conscience, and Hagen draws attention to the woodbird's song overhead and cunningly questions Siegfried about his knowledge of its language. It is, however, to enliven Gunther that Siegfried agrees to tell his boyhood's story, which he does with a plethora of appropriate *motifs* until the moment when (to the Forest Murmurs) he tasted the Dragon's blood and understood the woodbird's song. He sings its story of the treasure and the Ring, and the warning of the treachery of Mime, whom he killed. "Did the bird tell him anything else?" ask his enraptured hearers.

It is Hagen's cue: for oblivion blots from Siegfried's mind all recollection of Brünnhilde. He passes him a horn containing a draught which revives his memory: we hear the mysterious Tarn-helm theme, very softly, as Siegfried drinks, and in a rising happiness recalls the bird's tale of Brünnhilde, his destined bride, sleeping on the mountain surrounded by flames. In a wave of

Siegfried's Funeral March: Bayreuth, Wieland Wagner's production

entranced recollection he describes how he penetrated the flames
and awakened her; and he is unaware of the sensational effect on
his hearers until Hagen suddenly calls his attention to the fluttering
upward flight of Wotan's ravens, on wing to warn the God that
doom is near. As Siegfried turns to watch them Hagen, with a
savage cry of vengeance:

plunges a spear in his back. The stricken hero turns and makes
a mighty effort to fell Hagen with his shield, but collapses in the
attempt, while Gunther and four Vassals, who have hurled themselves on Hagen to restrain him, demand in horror the reason for
his action. "Retribution" is his curt reply: and morose and enigmatic as ever, his dark figure strides away across the horizon.

Gunther, who now realises something of his friend's innocence
and betrayal, kneels in grief beside him: and as is the way with
operatic heroes Siegfried has still some singing breath left before
he dies. Raising himself with an effort, he whispers Brünnhilde's
name as the harps recall her awakening, and indeed he poignantly,
in delirium, goes through the scene of their first meeting and
imagines her beckoning him as he dies. The Fate *motif* softly
accompanies his death, and in the magnificent Funeral March that
follows, as he is born aloft on his shield and carried in a cortège
across the horizon, Gunther grievingly following, all the *motifs* of
his life are spun into a musical texture of supreme·and sombre
grandeur. The majestic rhythm of the Death Melody itself is
thundered in a reverberating reiteration:

'Götterdämmerung': Hermann Uhde as Gunther

As an heroic elegy in sound it is unequalled in the whole of musical literature; and its moving effect in the theatre, as the cortège disappears into the mists of the Rhine, is unique.

Night descends, and we are back in the Hall of the Gibichungs for the final scene of the tragedy. Gutrune restlessly moves about the Hall: she has glimpsed Brünnhilde wandering towards the Rhine, and her heart is full of misgivings. When Hagen's horn and call are heard – not Siegfried's – her fears increase, and are not quelled by his cruel, jocular suggestion that she greet her hero, Siegfried, after the chase. The Hall suddenly fills with people carrying torches; Hagen brutally tells her Siegfried is dead, killed by a boar; and by the light of the flares Gutrune sees at last Siegfried on his bier. With a cry she falls on his body, and instinct tells her in her anguish that he was deliberately slain. She desperately accuses the unhappy Gunther of breaking his oath of brotherhood, and Gunther, himself sickened with shame and grief, declares that Hagen struck the blow. Hagen, reckless in triumph, admits it and declares the Ring on Siegfried's finger now belongs to him; and when Gunther, roused at last, tries to restrain him kills him at one blow. But terror now comes even to Hagen: for Siegfried's dead hand, with the Ring, is raised threateningly from the bier, and as all cower back Brünnhilde appears through the pillars, statuesque now, and supernaturally calm. She has heard from the Rhinemaidens the truth of Siegfried's innocence, and her voice is clear and tranquil as she commands the women to cease their wailing. The turmoil is suddenly stilled, and Gutrune's protests are quickly silenced by the truth. She had no right in Siegfried – his love was for Brünnhilde, as she now realises. A weak figure suddenly transformed, she curses Hagen for his plot that destroyed them all, and bends over the body of her slain and once-loved brother. So she fades from the scene, her *motif* sweet and pitiful in the orchestra to the last.

It is Brünnhilde alone who now commands the stage and, like some Olympian Goddess, as the Fate *motif* sounds, she begins the great Immolation scene – a soliloquy in music which is to wind together all the threads, musical and dramatic, of the story. She orders a pyre to be built by the Rhine and Siegfried's horse to be brought; and while this is done, transfigured by the recollection of their love, she sings a radiant panegyric of the dead hero. It changes to deep grief as she remembers the Gods, and invokes Wotan to see her suffering and the heavy burden he has laid on her, his once-loved daughter, by allowing the Curse of his own deeds to fall on Siegfried. But she has learnt wisdom, and in clairvoyance sees the end of the Gods, and that Wotan will at last find peace. "Rest, rest, O God": her farewell is a deep and moving elegy:

Now she takes the ring from Siegfried's finger, and sings to the Rhinemaidens that at last it will be returned to them, and the Curse ended: they can claim it from her own ashes, and melt it back into the original gold. She commands Wotan's ravens to fly back to him with her news, and seizing a burning brand flings it into the pyre on which Siegfried's body has been placed. Crying to Gräne that he is to meet his master, she mounts him and in a final glorious burst of song rides him into the flames.

And now the great conflagration rises to Valhalla itself, and the Gods too meet their destined 'twilight'. As the flames die the Rhine overflows its banks, and Hagen, making a last greedy clutch at the Ring, is pulled into the depths by the Rhinemaidens and drowned. Soon all is still: only the waves lap peacefully over the ruins of the abode of the Gibichungs, the majestic Valhalla *motif*, on bass trumpet and tubas, swells above the undulations of cellos, violas and harps, and at the very end of this extraordinarily beautiful and noble epilogue the theme of Redemption by Love – first heard in Sieglinde's rapturous "*O hehrstes Wunder*" – sings out radiantly on violins and flutes, as the waves ripple into silence.

Wagner's magical web of *motifs*, not only in this final scene but throughout *The Ring*, can only be sketched in this study, and indeed attempts to name each strand can be carried to ridiculous and unnecessary lengths. The *motifs* are so musically apt to character, atmosphere and situation that their rich and subtle variations cannot mask them, but only serve to heighten the dramatic-musical effect in the theatre. The listener will always be conscious of their general implication, matching so superbly the action on the stage. Wagner's mastery of his resources was now complete, and the gigantic cycle of *Der Ring des Nibelungen* remains a monument to his individual genius and the new development of music-drama. There is nothing like it in the history of music, and its effect in the opera house is still unique.

VI Tristan und Isolde

It was in December, 1854, that Wagner first wrote to Liszt of his project for an opera on the theme of Tristan and Isolde, and made it clear in his letter that he planned it as a monument to an ideal love which had never come his way in life. It was conceived, therefore, in both frustration and sublimation; and if the contact with Schopenhauer's *The World as. Will and Idea* enriched the first mood with the sombre intensity of the death-wish, and the brief unconsummated Wesendonck idyll enhanced the second, it is clear that the genius behind the work and its idea was Wagner's own, already formulated in essentials before these later influences entered his life.

The legend of Tristan of Lyonesse and the Irish princess Isolde Wagner found in Godfrey of Strassburg's unfinished thirteenth century epic, which in its turn derived from Thomas of Britanie and the Britannic books, or Anglo-Norman legends. Subsequent developments of the story Wagner materially ignored, and Godfrey's version he enormously simplified, drawing from it a fine dramatic essence and giving a psychological interpretation to a number of scenes which in the original are purely on the physical plane. Thus he entirely alters the meaning of the love potion – which in his version merely brings to the surface a passion already patently simmering beneath a love-hate relationship, and which his lovers drink in the mutual belief that they are taking a draught of poison which will end their lives. The love story is stripped of all accretions likely to detract from its idealistic nobility, including the character of the second Isolde – "Isolde of the white hands" – whom the original Tristan married in Brittany in a vain attempt to forget Isolde, Queen of Cornwall. We thus lose the 'theatrical' *motif* of the second Isolde's jealousy, which was responsible for

131

the death of the wounded Tristan – broken-hearted when he is told the approaching ship flies a black sail, not the white one promised if the Isolde he loves is aboard and coming to heal him. But 'theatricality' was just the quality Wagner was not aiming at in this work: it is more a love-symphony than an opera, its action packed in the revolutionary chromatic and polyphonic score, and in the drama of idyllic, ill-starred love concentrated in its two chief figures.

It would appear from his own writings that the originality of the *Tristan* score was not entirely involuntary, a natural development of his matured powers as a musician (indeed in *Siegfried* and *Götterdämmerung*, completed after it, the music, though superb, is of a different style). In a sense Wagner consciously forged a new instrument to express the fated quality of his love-poem and the introspective range of his personal thoughts and emotions – for there is no doubt this is the most 'personal' of his works, torn out of his own emotional experience and longing as well as his mature development as an artist. *Leitmotifs*, of course, are not unique to *Tristan;* but here they are fewer than in *The Ring*, and woven with endless variations into an orchestral accompaniment unlike anything that had been heard in opera before.

So close is the chromatic structure of the *Tristan* melodies (and the score is wonderfully melodic) to atonality, that the later development by Schönberg of the twelve-tone scale might be said almost directly to derive from it. *Tristan* is not atonal, and it is still based in nineteenth century romanticism in music; but its method of melodic progression by semi-tones was in truth the "music of the future", which Wagner's music was often called by both his disciples and enemies during his lifetime. At the same time it was the perfect instrument for the expression of the super-charged emotion and tragedy of the love story: nowhere in music can one find such a mournful note of heartache and unassuaged sorrow, as in the Preludes to Act I and Act III of this, Wagner's romantic masterpiece.

The Prelude to Act I sets the note: its wonderful web of sound was said by Wagner himself to express the frustrated desire of Tristan and Isolde for each other. The opening is a Confession of Love, the next two bars the Desire itself:

132

Both are recurring elements in the score, the Desire being first put into words by Isolde in her Act I lament of Tristan lost to her, as we shall see. (Another important *motif* heard in the Prelude is that depicting Tristan's 'Look' or 'Glance', again sung by Isolde in a key moment of the first act:)

The Love Potion (or Death Draught):   — 口之暑69(水)

[draft]

sounded first in the brass and afterwards in the woodwind (with a special concentration on the bass-clarinet), is as inevitable a thread in the fabric of the score; and so is the Deliverance by Death:

These are basic themes which are to take on many colours and changes in the opera and always return with dramatic appositeness and in the perfect tonal mood.

The curtain rises to show Isolde's pavilion erected on the deck of a ship at sea. Isolde, the Irish princess, is being taken by Tristan for a political marriage with his uncle, King Marke of Cornwall, and although we do not know as yet the background to this situation, Isolde's position on a couch, her face buried in the cushions, is eloquent of grief. Her maid, Brangäne, has lifted a curtain and looks out on to the deck. As the orchestral Prelude ceases we hear the unaccompanied voice of a young sailor aloft, sweetly and nostalgically lamenting the Irish girl whom he has left on shore. Its third and fourth phrases are to become identified

133

with the Sea:

and his words of mourning for his Irish love and the wild wind that bears him away:

lash Isolde as an unintended insult. She demands furiously of Brangäne where they are sailing, and on learning they are nearing land launches into a prolonged and tempestuous curse of the arrogant ship, calling on the winds and sea to sink her and end her troubles. Brangäne, lamenting Isolde's strange condition and silent, dry-eyed departure from her homeland, is forced to open the curtains at Isolde's demand for air. For the first time we see the rest of the ship with its knights and crew – Tristan standing silent and apart, with his friend Kurwenal at his feet. Again the voice of the sailor is heard in his bitter-sweet song, followed immediately by Isolde's deeply-felt exclamation at the sight of Tristan:

Fated to be hers yet lost to her – thus she broods on Tristan, to the tune we have already heard as the 'Desire' *motif* in the Prelude. Almost immediately it is followed by a cry in which she expresses her *fey** realisation of the fate of death which threatens Tristan's head and heart, so beloved of her:

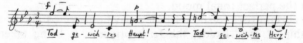

It is a Fate *motif* to be heard at many later points of the action, including the drinking of the love-potion and Isolde's extinguishing of the torch as a signal to her lover in Act II. But Isolde's mood changes to a forced scorn at Tristan's shamed fear to look at her

* She actually uses the word *feig*, which is a literal equivalent of the Scottish word *fey*, referring to a man near to death. The same expression occurs in Icelandic – the language of so many sagas on which northern poets, including Wagner, based their legends.

134

'Tristan und Isolde': Frida Leider as Isolde

– as she interprets his brooding, averted glance – and adds more in anger than sorrow that he is bringing a corpse as the bride he has won for his master. In a proud musical gesture, its plunging intervals characteristic of her in this scene, she bids Brangäne tell Tristan that she commands his presence:

But although Brangäne walks up to the stern and gives Isolde's message, Tristan is non-committal and Kurwenal mockingly sings a jovial ballad about the defeat of Isolde's Irish *fiancé*, Morold, by the Cornish hero Tristan. The sailors take up the theme and Brangäne can only return to the raging Isolde, and repeat Tristan's own courageous but firm reply that he cannot leave the helm: how otherwise can he pilot the ship bringing the "pearl of womanhood" to King Marke?

It is a lash to Isolde who bitterly repeats it. And in a great narration we now at last hear the full story. Tristan had indeed freed Cornwall from its tribute to Ireland by slaying Morold, the Irish hero, but wounded had drifted back to land after putting to sea and under the name of 'Tantris' been succoured by the unsuspecting Isolde. To her, skilled in herbal magic like her mother, he owed the healing of his wound, as she tenderly recalls:

But finding a notch in his sword exactly fitting the piece found in Morold's death wound, she realises he is the killer of her betrothed, and raises the sword to slay him in revenge. But the sword drops from her hand as she meets Tristan's 'glance', forcing her to realise her own love for the sick man, and suspect his own for her:

This 'look' of Tristan's, piercing her heart, is a key *motif* in the whole work, and one on which she lingers now with a poignant tenderness. But tenderness turns again to rage and wounded pride when she relates how, in spite of his protested love, he returned to Cornwall and came back to claim her as bride for his uncle. It was a political match of such value that Tristan had probably, out of loyalty to King Marke, suppressed his own feelings; but to Isolde, a woman as well as a princess, it is a deep betrayal of herself and her country, once so strong that it had been able to exact taxes from Cornwall. Her anguish is expressed in a bitterly sarcastic mimicry of Tristan's supposed pointing out of her as a prize to King Marke, and a curse of Tristan which again with plunging intervals thrills above the stave like ice. In vain Brangäne tries to comfort her and turn Tristan's recommendation of her to Marke as a queen into a compliment. Isolde betrays where her own heart lies, and to Brangäne comes the thought of the casket Isolde's mother, skilled in magic, had given her on leaving. Among

136

its herbal draughts is a love-potion; but when Isolde calls for the casket it is a deadlier potion she seeks. As she seizes it, to Brangäne's horror, the chorus of sailors show land is sighted, and Kurwenal brings the news in a lusty, folk-like melody. Isolde calmly orders him to bring Tristan to her, and tell him plainly she will not land and become Marke's bride until he has come, so that she may ask his forgiveness for her attitude on the voyage.

Kurwenal goes grumpily enough (he seems to suspect the hold Isolde has on Tristan; and his resentment is perhaps tinged with a friend's jealousy). The ruse works; but before Tristan appears Isolde commands Brangäne to prepare the poison, and is unaware that the loving and terrified maid has substituted the love-potion in its place.

Tristan's entrance gives a new dynamic shift to the drama, and the orchestra sombrely underlines it. He stands quite still, pale and moody, and to Isolde's query as to why he has kept away from her on the voyage replies briefly that it is the custom when a knight escorts a bride for another. His maddening reticence and distant bearing enrage Isolde, and she makes it clear she has never ceased to wish to avenge Morold's death: to which Tristan makes a gloomy and revealing response: was Morold, then, so dear to her? But Isolde does not see the subtle psychological revelation, the pang of jealousy: she is too obsessed with the love-hate complex on her side. And, blind himself to anything but her apparent hatred, Tristan offers her his sword with which to kill him.

It is the second time she cannot do it. Beginning to realise the

Hans Hotter as Marke   *Jean de Reszke as Tristan*

true nature of their feelings, the fated pair exchange a long glance, and when Isolde suggests a drink of forgetfulness to heal their enmity and forgive all wrongs between them, Tristan at once intuitively realises her true meaning. He takes the goblet without question, and before he drains it sounds a note on his honour, anguish and loyalty ('truth') to King Marke we are to hear again, inverted, in Marke's later lament:

Before he can finish the draught Isolde snatches the cup from him and drinks herself; and in the long, harrowing pause in which the two wait for death their eyes meet and acknowledge at last the truth of their subconscious passion. Finally, too overcome to wonder at the stayed hand of death, they cry each other's names and fall into a fervent embrace. As they do so, the sailors' greeting of King Marke rends the air, but in their mutual joy they are unconscious of it and of Brangäne's sudden fear of what she has done. Isolde hardly notices her maid robing her royally to meet the King, and Tristan is too bemused to understand Kurwenal's announcement of his approach on a bark. At last the fainting Isolde begins to understand, and Tristan supports her as people crowd on the deck.

The second act takes place in the garden of King Marke's castle in Cornwall. A burning torch stands at the open door, and the sound of receding hunting horns floats with mysterious beauty from the distance:

To Isolde, listening, they are the symbol of her meeting with Tristan: for it is the royal hunt that takes the King away on the summer evening, and the quenching of the torch is to be the signal for her lover's approach.

In the orchestral introduction to this act we have already heard her ardent impatience, graphic in music:

138

Lilli Lehmann as Isolde

and before this, in the opening two bars, the *motif* of Day (enemy of the lovers who can only meet by night), which is to be a theme of their great love duet:

Brangäne now finds it impossible to instil caution and check Isolde's impatience till the sound of the horns has vanished. She warns her that Melot alone of the King's followers had watched her closely when she received him, pale and almost fainting, at the end of the voyage, and he suspects her meetings with Tristan. Isolde cannot or will not hear: she throws the torch to the ground and as its light gutters out her 'impatience' theme rises in momentum, below its flicker of violins. Tristan fails at first to appear, but does so at last as she waves her scarf, and the lovers fall into each other's arms, their hearts seeming to beat breathlessly in the music in a hurried, ecstatic verbal exchange.

. Practically the whole of this act is, in fact, a love duet, broken only by Brangäne's haunting warning sung off-stage from the tower, where she watches with foreboding for the return of the hunters. The 'Day' theme soon appears, with Tristan's regret of the light that so harshly parts them, and as they at last unclasp their embrace and move to a flowery bank, where Tristan sinks to his knees beside Isolde and rests his head on her arm, a melody expands between them which is a beautiful expression of gratitude to the night:

140

Brangräne's warning, floating from the distance in lovely mezzo-soprano tones, goes unheeded and the lovers' metaphor of night and day becomes an allegorical death-wish: night attracts them like death as the only true fulfilment of a love like theirs. They feel immortality within them, a feeling which is to reach its spiritual apex in Isolde's *Liebestod* (as Wagner himself named it) at the end of the opera. And when Kurwenal rushes on to break their self-absorption, followed by King Marke, his retainers and the treacherous Melot who has warned the King, Tristan characteristically utters only one sentence, the hopeless and resigned "*Der öde Tag zum letzten Mal*" (The dreary day comes for the last time).

Through all this scene he stands immobile, shielding the shamed Isolde from sight with his cloak. Marke's long expostulation, a lament at Tristan's disloyalty and broken friendship, is tedious only if inadequately sung: a noble bass voice capable of emotion and sensitivity can reveal a sorrowing beauty in the music, and one of its themes penetrates poignantly into Hans Sachs' musings in *Die Meistersinger*. Tristan makes no effort to defend himself: he turns only to Isolde and asks her if she is ready to accompany him to 'the dark land of night' where his mother went so soon after his own birth. Isolde understands he means death and assents immediately, but even as Tristan imprints a token kiss on her forehead Melot rushes on him. Tristan draws his sword, and bitterly remarks of his betrayer, "This was my friend" – but when Melot attacks he deliberately drops his guard and is run through. Isolde and Kurwenal rush to support the wounded man and the curtain quickly falls.

The Prelude to Act III is a monument to fatalistic melancholy, touching notes of aching sorrow rarely heard in music. Its opening, with ascending thirds on the violins, pervades the whole orchestral passage and much of the act that follows:

'*Tristan und Isolde*': setting for Act III by Leslie Hurry, Covent Garden production

Tristan has been carried to his birthplace, the castle of Kareol in Brittany, by Kurwenal, who tends his wounded friend and has come to realise that only 'the distant healer', Isolde, can save his life. He has put Tristan on a couch in the derelict garden, under the shade of a great lime tree, where he can watch the horizon of the sea for the ship carrying Isolde (to whom a message has been sent).

As the curtain rises the Prelude dies away and a new note is heard – a shepherd's pipe playing a haunting little folk-like tune (in fact, a *cor anglais* solo):

It is a lay Tristan has often heard in childhood, "the plaintive lay". The shepherd enters and speaks to Kurwenal, watching over the sleeping Tristan, and we learn his lay will change to one of joy if he sights the ship. Now, there is nothing, and he departs playing his sad lay.

142

Tristan now awakes and asks where he is: he is confused and unconvinced by Kurwenal's tender attempts at jovial optimism, hiding his own secret fear and grief. In the long monologue which constitutes almost the whole of this act – a supreme test of stamina for the tenor – Tristan passes through several phases of delirium. He believes he has been wandering in the land of night, which beckons him still with its happy oblivion; his yearning for Isolde is expressed in frequent cries of her name; he is obsessed by tangled thoughts on love and death, night and day, echoes from the previous act; and when he learns from Kurwenal that Isolde has been sent for, he is overcome with a feverish joy and the moved recognition of all his loyal friend has done for him. In his delirium he believes he sees Isolde's ship; but the mournful pipe of the shepherd disillusions Kurwenal, and Tristan himself wonders bitterly, "Is this the fate for which my mother bore me and died?" His mind wanders restlessly over the past, and fastens with a crazed horror on "the terrible drink". For a moment, as he collapses from the strain, Kurwenal believes him dead; but again Tristan revives and faintly asks after the ship, and his cry of 'Isolde' takes on a new yearning beauty:

Again he imagines he sees the ship, and this time to Kurwenal's incredulous joy the changed tune of the shepherd's pipe, "the

Wieland Wagner's production at Bayreuth: Act III

merry lay", confirms it:

It is interesting to note here that Tristan asks what flag the ship is flying, and when Kurwenal answers it is a 'bright' one he radiantly realises Isolde is on board: a strange slip on Wagner's part, for he has not otherwise included the story of the black and white flag of the legend, and the reference is unintelligible unless one knows this. For some dreadful moments it seems the ship will break on the rocks, but when Kurwenal tells Tristan she is safe Tristan impatiently sends him to the watch tower.

What Kurwenal fears then happens: in his ecstasy Tristan cannot keep still as his friend has begged him. Remembering the wounded Morold he deliriously tears the bandages from his own wound (it is a curious subconscious return of the death-wish) and staggers to meet Isolde, who must once again heal him. As she appears he falls in her arms and dies, her name on his lips. She gives a tiny, soft cry on F sharp, and her lovely swan-song is a prelude to the later *Liebestod*, often overlooked through the greater fame of the opera's final melody.

When Marke and Brangäne appear she is apparently already dead, and remains inert through the confusion in which Kurwenal, thinking the new intruders mean harm to Tristan, slays Melot and is himself mortally wounded by Marke's followers – returning to die at his friend's side. But Brangäne has told Marke the true story of the love potion, and the King's lament is now for the 'true friend' he had come, too late, to forgive. Then only Isolde raises herself and over Tristan's body breathes the celestial phrases of her *Liebestod* (Love in Death), which like Brünnhilde's more heroic Immolation weaves together the major strands in the music-drama. Much like the lyrical '*O hehrstes Wunder*' of Sieglinde which we hear again in the finale to *Götterdämmerung*, the most shining thread in Isolde's mystic salute to love's immortality is the radiant:

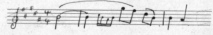

a phrase we have first heard her sing in the Love Duet. The *Liebestod* opens gently and plaintively:

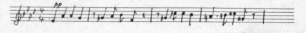

Sylvia Fisher as Isolde

撕開的面紗

It is a ripped veil between life and death in which Isolde imagines that Tristan's eyes are opening and he is smiling at her, and in this radiance of immortality she remains trance-like until the final soft *arpeggios* in the orchestra, when she joins Tristan in death.

"The happenings are all of a delicate, intimate nature; every quiver of the face, every movement of the eyes, must tell its tale..." This emphasis by Wagner himself, in a letter to King Ludwig, on the psychological intimacy of the drama, is worth recording, for it is not always observed in production, which tends often to give a symbolic heroism alien to the nature of this most lyric of Wagner's later dramas. In a small opera house, such as the story really requires, there is, however, the difficulty of the huge orchestral score overwhelming the singers, a difficulty Wagner himself found insuperable at the Residenz Theatre in Munich, and which reinforced his longing for an orchestra placed under the stage – an ambition achieved later at Bayreuth.

At Bayreuth today Wagner's grandson, Wieland, has produced this opera, like others of Wagner, in a purely symbolic setting with a gauze curtain between singers and audience. But it is worth reflecting that a major force in Wagner's works is the often subtle characterisation, and if modern production, however beautiful, obscures this and the acting of the singers, a great deal of dramatic relevance is lost and Wagner's genius inevitably flawed. The ideal fusion of the music-drama he visualised has perhaps never been realised on the stage: our taste, rightly in some ways, is today for a less realistic, more imaginative approach. It is imperative, nevertheless, that the characters retain their profound human attributes, and the balance of music and drama, about which Wagner felt so passionately, is observed. For his characters are of all time, as the hold of Tristan and Isolde, like Shakespeare's Romeo and Juliet, on the minds of each new generation proves.

145

VII Die Meistersinger

That Wagner, in the full maturity of his genius, was able to produce a comedy opera in which the music buds and flowers with a spring-like profusion, would seem a miracle but for the technical mastery we know he had by now achieved, and the youthful energy and gaiety of which his nature was capable long into middle age, and which no artistic struggles and hardships seemed ever entirely to quench. He was, of course, as incapable as his admirer Shaw of writing a comedy without philosophical content; and if the lashing of the traditionalist Beckmesser (inspired by the anti-Wagnerian critic Eduard Hanslick) descends at moments to downright farce, Hans Sachs is a humanist figure in whom a mellowed philosophy still contains flashes of bitterness at the madness of a world at strife.

It was on the 16th of July, 1845, that Wagner, during that most productive holiday at Marienbad, first sketched out a scenario for an opera on Hans Sachs and the mediaeval guild of Mastersingers at Nuremberg. He had been reading Gervinus' *History of German Literature*, which reminded him of the homely German poet and song-writer, Sachs; but he could hardly have been ignorant, too, of the opera on Sachs and the Mastersingers composed by Lortzing (light opera composer of the ever-popular *Czar und Zimmermann*) and produced only five years before. Nothing came of Wagner's sketch, however, until January, 1862, when his thoughts once again returned to the subject and he completed the poem in thirty days. The overture was ready for performance, including the principal *motifs*, in April, 1862, but it was not until

←— 'Die Meistersinger': Rudolf Bockelmann as Hans Sachs

'Die Meistersinger': Prinz-Regenten Theater, Munich, 1901. Setting for Act I

February, 1867, that the opera was completed, apparently with a good deal of revision of the original poem to meet the demands of the music now cascading through Wagner's brain: for we find Wagner writing to King Ludwig: "one of these days I shall have to write the words of Walther's Prize Song, the melody of which is already finished". The opera was, of course, first performed at Munich in 1868, but Liszt heard the full score played at Triebschen in October, 1867, and wrote to Princess Wittgenstein: "I was amazed by the incomparable sap, audacity, vigour, abundance, verve and mastery of the *Meistersinger*. No one but he could have produced such a masterpiece".

Although he was depressed when he began serious work on it, Wagner turns, in *Die Meistersinger*, from the sorrows of *Tristan* as if to a revivifying spring. None today would contest Liszt's immediate reaction. And one of the miracles of the score is its use not only of the advanced technical style Wagner had now achieved, but of the Bach contrapuntal and earlier *chorale* forms which seemed to the composer to be nearer to the period of the story, without restricting his musical style to archaic mediaeval structures.

The melancholy of *Tristan* is of course transformed here into brighter major keys, and the Overture begins and ends in an un-clouded C major. Its opening theme of the Mastersingers them-selves – not the romantic troubadours of earlier chivalry, as in *Tannhäuser*, but honest burghers and citizens keeping music alive

148

and Act II

in their own city – is vigorous and ebullient:

After a lively development this theme gives way to a *motif* marked '*espressivo*', which throughout the score we are to come to associate with the 'awakening love' of Walther and Eva:

Then lyricism again gives way to the brilliant fanfare of the Mastersingers, sometimes known as 'The Banner' *motif*:

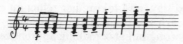

only to melt later into our first introduction, on the violins (*dolcissimo ed espress.*) and with the first change of key, to Walther's Prize Song, a melody to be heard many times fluidly in the score, until it crystallises into its final form in the last act:

149

These are to be the most important repetitive threads in the musical fabric, but even in the Overture Wagner's instrumental use of them shows a superb craftsmanship, with a delicate use of woodwind, as well as violins and brass, which is a feature of the whole work.

The Overture flows into the opening scene, the Church of St. Katharine, in which the last few seats of the nave are visible. Here sit Eva and her chaperone Magdalene – the lovely girl furtively exchanging glances with a handsome young knight, Walther von Stolzing, who stands by a pillar. The music has melted into a Chorale of Baptism, harmonised in the manner of Bach, with organ:

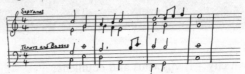

But beneath it we hear snatches of the Awakening of Love *motif* and the Prize Song, as the lovers exchange their speaking glances. As the service ends Eva sends Magdalene back to the pew on various pretexts, while Walther, who has met Eva the night before in her father, Pogner's, house, tries to press a response to his ardour from the girl. The interest is obviously mutual and we soon become aware of another attraction of a similar kind – between Magdalene and David, the gay, good-natured young apprentice of Hans Sachs, who bustles in to help prepare the hall for the coming meeting of Mastersingers.

Magdalene has already told Walther that Pogner has promised Eva's hand to the winner of the annual song contest to be held in the meadows next day, and taking her reluctant charge away has left Walther to learn the rules of the Mastersingers from David. David is not only song but shoemaking apprentice to Hans Sachs, acknowledged leader of the Mastersingers, and his elaborate instructions as to the various modes and styles are somewhat confused between the two trades, as Walther soon realises with baffled amusement. But one vital thing he does learn – the rank of Master can be attained only by composing a poem in a new metre to a new tune, and this he sets his heart on doing.

David's instructions are not only witty but charmingly composed; we hear fragments of Sachs' own robust Act II song while cobbling Beckmesser's shoes:

and little melodies more lyrically connected with the actual business of song-construction. It is a light tenor part which can always be beguiling and mischievous in the right hands, a contrast to Walther's more heroic lyrical tenor and graver personality.

Through all this the apprentices have been preparing the hall; David is officially commanding operations but their jollity is not without a great deal of banter of him, both as regards his master's punishments and his well-known fancy for the older Magdalene. Their chirping chorus ceases respectfully, however, when the Mastersingers appear, and we soon realise the town clerk Beckmesser, a bachelor, is the likeliest winner: a dry rule-keeper, no longer young, now eagerly pressing for Pogner's help. Pogner, to whom the art of the Mastersingers is of prime importance, warns him and the Mastersingers nevertheless that the first choice is Eva's: he will not force his daughter to wed the winner against her will, although in that case she must remain unmarried.*

Walther is greeted by Pogner with pleasure, as Beckmesser notes with agitated jealousy, and the young knight from the country makes known his wish to become a Master and take part in the contest. He is asked to name his own Master, and in a charming song, "*Am stillen herd*", confesses he learned by the fireside, during the winter snows, from the book of the minstrel Walther von der Vogelweide, and from the inspiration of Nature itself:

It is a strange story to his hearers, hidebound by the rules of their guild; but it is decided Beckmesser shall be 'marker' (seven mistakes only are allowed) and the burgher Kothner, to a very jolly tune riddled with 'orthodox' trills and *fioritura*, explains the rules.

Walther feels himself rather bullied, and Beckmesser's spite is manifest; but the knight sits as required and again sings a song,

* This odd echo of Egeus and the Athenian law was probably borrowed by Wagner from *A Midsummer Night's Dream*. But it sits rather uneasily on his comedy and on the character of Pogner, one of those noble Wagnerian basses who, apart from this unexpectedly harsh decision, seems a kind father with a call on our sympathy.

151

full of the joys of love and the spring:

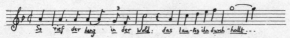

It is interrupted freely by the vindictive scratching of Beckmesser's chalk and the bewilderment of the Mastersingers on seeing the marked 'mistakes', but Sachs, who has already shown his broader tolerance by urging Pogner and the Mastersingers to let the populace themselves decide the winner on the morrow, now further reveals his freedom from prejudice by praising Walther's song. The best music is not restricted by rules and the judgment of the technicians: it has a universal appeal that must not be despised, and makes its own rules and keeps to them. This he feels in Walther's freer form of expression. His expostulation, and Walther's defiance, go unheeded and the Mastersingers depart in an uproar augmented by the dancing mockery of the apprentices. But Sachs remains, a lonely, dignified figure, reflecting on the song and the genuine love for Eva he feels in it. A widower with a taciturn affection for the beautiful girl, his renunciation stems from this moment: he acknowledges without bitterness the call of youth to youth.

The second act takes place on the evening of the same day. The Nuremberg street is flanked by two houses, Sachs' and Pogner's. In front of Sachs' is an elder (or lilac) tree, of Pogner's a lime tree. The short Prelude brightly sets the atmosphere of a summer night – Midsummer's Eve, the Feast of St. John – and the bustling apprentices are once again taunting David in lively chorus. Magdalene in passing learns from him of Walther's ill-success, and attributing this to the youth's failure to give him good counsel petulantly withholds the basket of delicacies with which she apparently has, in the past, captivated the apprentice's heart. Pogner and Eva then appear and sit beneath the lime tree: musically their scene is brief but tenderly beautiful. Pogner half-thinks of calling on Sachs, whose work-light shows in the window: he is troubled about the quarrel earlier in the day, and given not a little food for thought when Eva, reminded of the joys in store for her tomorrow, asks merely if he saw Walther at the church hall. Still troubled, he is induced to go indoors, while Eva learns from Lene the catastrophic news – only sharpened by the rumour that Beckmesser, dubious of his chances, is coming to serenade her.

As they go indoors the interest shifts again to Sachs: he has

153

← *Herman Winkelmann (the original Parsifal at Bayreuth, 1882) as Walter von Stolzing*

Ernestine Schumann-Heink as Magdalene   *Victoria de los Angeles as Eva*

commanded David (sufficiently distracted by the loss of Lene's tasties and perhaps affection) to put his bench outside under the elder tree, so he can work at Beckmesser's new shoes in the warm summer air. He muses now among the elder's scent, mellowly and with a nostalgic sweetness. He wishes he could think only of his cobbling and forget the poetry and song forever disturbing his mind. Walther's song, and his own feeling for Eva, invade his thoughts, and once again he realises the narrowness of musical rules, and the genius behind Walther's inspiration, learned from Nature. Wagner himself, of course, is here: the whole opera, in one sense, crystallises his own appalling fight for recognition, for the truth of his own new rules and inspiration, harried by the mockery and spite of the critics and certain musicians. (It is worth noting here that Sachs' earlier references to the good taste of the public and the 'universal' appeal of great music are also torn from Wagner's own experience: in theatres the musical public acclaimed his works long before the general run of musicologists and critics.)

Eva now comes to Sachs and a bitter-sweet scene ensues. The girl herself is confused in mind: she had thought she loved Sachs and gently challenges him as to why he, an eligible widower, is allowing her to fall into the hands of Beckmesser without entering a master-song of his own. But she is *distrait*, too, and Sachs soon realises it is news of Walther that draws her to him. He has his silent pang, and when Walther appears decides to help the lovers if he can. But Walther, in despair at the morning's proceedings, urges Eva to elope with him and the girl, carried away by passion, agrees. Running into the house, she returns in Magdelene's clothes (Magdelene, in Eva's, is to watch for Beckmesser from Eva's window).

Sachs, who has overheard, believes such a plan would be fatal, and to prevent the lovers' escape throws the beam of his lamp across the street. And the appearance of Beckmesser, ludicrous with a be-ribboned lute, traps them still further. They can only hide in the darkness until Beckmesser departs.

In spite of Sachs' lusty hammering he shows no signs of doing so. After a wrangle, it is agreed Sachs shall tap the shoes only at his mistakes, and it is with rising fury (stimulated by the cobbler's own genial good humour) that Beckmesser finds himself singing his serenade against a veritable shower of marker's blows. The serenade is a witty enough gibe of Wagner's at what might be called the *coloratura* tripe of Italian opera in his period, the plucked lute-strings floridly punctuating the pedantic rule of time. Sachs' own song, a biblical *double entendre* on the casting of Eve out of Paradise (the references to Eva naturally madden Beckmesser), is jovial and rhythmic in the real Sachs' own style of composition:

Wieland Wagner's Bayreuth production of 'Die Meistersinger' Act II

It is preceded by a rousing refrain, giving fine scope to the higher range of the bass-baritone singer:

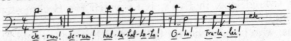

The noise not unexpectedly awakes the neighbours; and as shutters begin to open and night-capped heads appear, David, also looking out, recognises Magdalene at the window opposite, listening to Beckmesser's serenade. Furious with jealousy, he rushes out and starts beating the unfortunate (and mistaken) wooer with a stick – and as apprentices and burghers rush into the street a brawl begins of heroic magnitude, not quenched by the jugs of water poured by indignant wives on the fighters below. It is marvellously set by Wagner in fugal style – a massive piece of contrapuntal writing in which all the individual characters and chorus take part.

Yet his final stroke of genius remains for the end. The entry of the Night Watchman, instrument of the Law, scatters the belligerents: suddenly all is hushed and still. The Watchman rubs his eyes at the sight of the miraculously emptied street. Only his voice now sounds in the scented night air:

The moon beams gently on the peaceful scene, the instrument of the Law blows his horn, and the curtain falls to music mischievously soft and innocent.

The last act shows us first the interior of Sachs' house. It is St. John's Day morning, and in the sadly beautiful Prelude we have heard the shoemaker's reflective and lonely thoughts, so close to certain themes in *Tristan* for a reason we shall see:

In the rather over-done and slightly crazy game of '*motif*-naming' this has been called Sachs' 'Profound Emotion': we are to hear it much later, for it is the root of his resigned renunciation of Eva. We hear, too, among familiar themes the *chorale* set to the historical Sachs' own words, "*Wach auf, es nahet gen den Tag*" (Awake! The dawn of day is breaking).

156

When the curtain rises we find him reading by a window. David enters, with a basket of food given by Magdalene as a peace-offering, and fears his master's anger at the fracas of the night before. Yet it is obvious Sachs, absorbed, hardly hears his stumbling apologies. He asks the boy only to sing the poem prepared for St. John's Day, and after an amusing initial mistake (David begins with the theme of Beckmesser's serenade, still running in his head from the previous night), we listen charmed to the clear young voice, proud of its accomplishment, in the folk-like tune:

Half-way through, at the word 'Hans', he realises it is also Sachs' nameday, and in a burst of generosity offers him a cherished sausage from his basket.

Sachs smilingly refuses and, when the boy has left, breaks into the great monologue, *'Wahn! Wahn!'* which is the profound philosophical climax of the opera. 'In a flash of vision', Neville Cardus has written, "Sachs (or rather Wagner) sees in Nürnberg's momentary madness a microcosm of the greater world". It is one of those moments of shaken faith in God and humanity, of appalled brooding on human propensity to war and strife, that illuminate passages of most great writers and tear the minds of people of natural goodness, intelligence and tolerance. Sachs can only explain the night's madness by the magic of the elder's scent and midsummer eve; the tumult in the music sweetens and softens on the violins at his thought. He prays the madness may be put to use – the ruffling of placidity bring sharper awareness, and perhaps acknowledgement of the nobler aspects of art.

As if at the thought, Walther – whom Sachs had dragged into his house out of the turmoil the preceding night – now appears. A dream still obsesses his waking thoughts, and Sachs encourages him to sing of it and put it into coherent form. The stanzas that follow expand at last the glowing melody of the Prize Song *motif* already heard in snatches, and Sachs, taking it down in his note-book, knows that here is the master-song. He helps the knight to polish his work and begs him to remember both dream-poem and melody in the day's festival of song.

When they go out Wagner creates a brilliant comic contrast in the orchestra. For Beckmesser, groaning from his beating, appears, and as he limps about the room the orchestra humorously under-lines his painful memories and agitation with appropriate musical

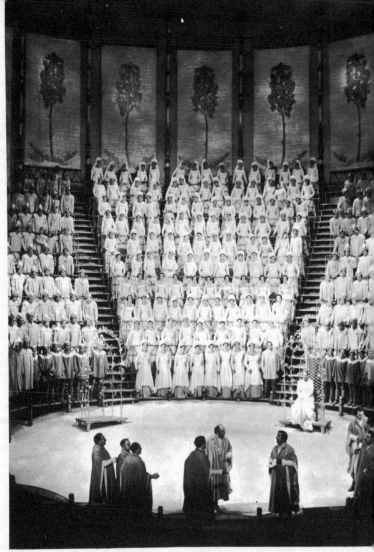

'*Die Meistersinger*' *Act III: production by Wieland Wagner, Bayreuth*

echoes. We hear a snatch of the Prize Song as his eye alights on Sachs' notes. Now at last he speaks, furious at what he believes to be Sachs' underhand intention of entering the contest with a song of his own. When Sachs surprises him stealing the notes the shoemaker, however, is astonishingly amiable. Rather than make Beckmesser a thief, he says ironically, he will give the poem to him:

he has no intention of using it himself. Delighted at having a song by the master to win him the prize (for Sachs pledges his silence) the unfortunate clerk hurries away. But Sachs knows this pedant incapable of doing justice to such an original poem, and for once the kind and tolerant humanist looks forward to the disaster of one who has shown only malice in love and art.

He is disturbed now by Eva, radiantly dressed for the festival, and about whose complaints of a pinching shoe he soon has his suspicions. These are confirmed when Walther enters and the girl listens ardently to the third stanza of his Prize Song, which her presence has inspired. But the immediate reaction afterwards is revealing and touching: the girl bursts into tears on Sachs' breast and admits she had wished to choose *him* this day. Yet she has no choice – her love for Walther is spontaneous, and too strong for her will. Sachs explains gently that he understands only too well: he has been reading the tale of Tristan and Isolde, he adds wryly, and has no wish to play the part of King Marke. This passage, strangely moving, is marked with actual *Tristan* quotations in the orchestra – both of the lovers' 'Desire' and King Marke's troubled grief. But psychologically, Sachs also is not flatly drawn: his own poignant feelings he tends to hide in outbursts of pointed irritation about people never being satisfied with his shoemaking. Yet when Magdalene and David enter he makes David a journeyman – his apprenticeship ended – genially enough with a formal box on the ear, and the five present, the two pairs of lovers and lonely philosopher, join in a luminous Quintet which has long been recognised as a peak of Wagner's genius.

Eva, always exquisitely represented in music, has the serene and dulcet opening line:

The shining beauty of this 'set piece' of voices, so unusual in Wagner's later works, lingers in our ears as the singers depart, David only remaining behind to lock up Sachs' shop.

There is no break in the music when the curtain falls, only the fanfare of distant horns shattering the radiant tranquillity of the Quintet; and when the curtains open again it is on the scene of the Song Festival outside the walls of the city, gaily bedecked with flowers and banners, while the people, in holiday attire, excitedly move and chatter. The guilds of the tradesmen appear in turn

159

with their banners and individual song, and then the apprentices engage the girls in a lively and popular waltz, beginning softly:

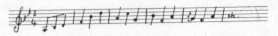

This is broken up by the arrival of the Mastersingers to their resplendent march, and as they sit on the raised dais provided the crowd burst spontaneously into a *chorale* of honour to Hans Sachs: his own "*Wach auf, es nahet gen den Tag*" which we have heard in the Act III Prelude:

Sachs' reply is preceded by the theme of his 'Emotion'. He is, in fact, deeply moved, but he asks only that the people will honour the art of the festival, and Pogner who cares for this art so much that he has given his greatest treasure, his daughter, to encourage interest in its preservation.

Beckmesser is the first contestant and the crowd greet him with dubious looks which turn to delirious mockery when, fumbling in nerves and memory, he makes the expected nonsense of Walther's poem (sung inappropriately to the tune of his previous night's serenade). The clerk waspishly accuses Sachs of its authorship, but Sachs quietly says the real poet will sing it to them and reveal its true nature. Walther now steps forward, to a murmur of admiration at his appearance, and the lovely air of the Prize Song floats in the summer sunlight, entrancing his hushed hearers. Yet when he is offered the prize and crown, from Eva's own hands, his bitterness at the Mastersingers breaks forth and he refuses them.

It is Sachs now who persuades him in a great panegyric of German art, which guilds such as those of the Mastersingers help to preserve. If their land is invaded, and the Holy Roman Empire destroyed, it is through them alone that the nation's culture can survive.

It is a noble form of patriotism with which artists of all lands can feel in key: Wagner's sympathies were always with the common German people and their national artistic heritage, and his passion

160

here is absolutely divorced from the type of Prussian-Nazi social and military ideal into which his works have sometimes been perverted by others. This final salute of Sachs to German art is a moving expression of faith, and a profoundly-felt belief of Wagner the musician. No opera could have a spiritually finer conclusion than this; and after it the crowd do choral homage to Sachs while Eva places the garland on Walther's head.

We use 'comedy' of this work for want of a better word; but its fountain of melody and verse has deeper springs, like some comedies of Shakespeare – musically and often in thought its radiance is shaded by profound emotion and an artist's philosophy of life.

Tiana Lemnitz as Eva

'Parsifal' Act I, Covent Garden 1951.

Ludwig Weber (right) as Gurnemanz, Sigurd Bjørling as Amfortas

VIII Parsifal

Wagner's last opera, *Parsifal* (until late in its composition he used the earlier spelling Parzifal), was in a sense a synthesis of the religious and mythical forces which throughout his life provided the yeast to his creative impulse. Longer even than *The Ring* in coming to fruition, its theme first began to work on his imagination as early as July, 1845, when he read Wolfram von Eschenbach's poem, *Parzifal*, as a preparation for his own *Lohengrin*. Two years before this, he had composed the short cantata or 'biblical scene', *Das Liebesmahl der Apostel* ("The Holy Supper of the Apostles"), and in 1848 he planned a drama, *Jesus of Nazareth*, which like a Buddhist story, *Die Sieger* ("The Victors"), some years later, was eventually abandoned as the source of a future opera. Both, however, occupied his mind for many years alongside *Parsifal*, and elements of them were finally absorbed into the opera, with its strange yet powerful symbol of pure Christian love and innocence superseding the seductive paganism of the Saracen. The Mary Magdalene element in Kundry's schizophrenic nature comes from *Jesus of Nazareth*, and the Buddhist transmigration of souls, or theory of reincarnation, also inspires the conception of the same enigmatic character (Klingsor's "Herodias thou wert, and who besides?" is a revealing key to Kundry's complex symbolism in the second act).

Kundry shows Wagner's dramatic and creative imagination at its supreme height: deeper in her psychological and religious implications than the 'Holy Fool' Parsifal, the Satanic Klingsor and the suffering sinner Amfortas, she binds together Venus and Elisabeth, the simple symbols of profane and sacred love in Wagner's earlier *Tannhäuser*, and brings a new Christian depth and complexity to the whole conception of womanhood and humanity in the artist's mind. Her legendary basis in the Parsifal story was twofold: Kondrie, the sorceress, and Orgeluse, the seductress. With a fine stroke of dramatic economy (noticeable throughout in his use of the character) Wagner fused this evil pair into one, but how richly his artistic stature had increased since the creation of Ortrud in *Lohengrin* is shown in the spiritual conflicts that emerge in Kundry, making her at once a problematical yet closely integrated personality; a concentrated fusion of demon and angel and a human being 'heightened', as all the great figures of tragedy from Greek drama onwards are 'heightened', by a suffering and confusion of instincts more deeply accented than in life, yet essentially rooted in it. She is not only sorceress and seductress, woman spiritual and profane. She is also Mary Magdalene, the sinner redeemed, an almost inevitable intruder in this close Christian allegory, and she is also, by a stroke of inspiration, a feminine equivalent of the legendary Ahasuerus, the Wandering Jew, who insulted Christ on His way to the Crucifixion and was doomed to roam the earth (as Wagner's not dissimilar Flying Dutchman roamed the seas) through generations of lives before he found penitence, death and redemption.

Atmospherically the Ahasuerus parallel worked magnificently, bringing in the colour of Kundry's Arabian connections; and the effect of the Christ-episode in the development of her character was profound – leading naturally to the Magdalene-like transformation of the last scene, the mocking and fatal laughter (an echo of Aha-

Fritz Wolff as Parsifal, Act I

suerus' mocking of Christ) which bursts forth to destroy her at every climax in her life, and the fascination to her of Parsifal, the Christ-figure for whom her restless spirit has been sent on its everlasting quest for redemption. The Ibsen-like technique of gradual revelation used by Wagner in building up this background is a remarkable example of his maturity as a dramatist; and if *Parsifal* is the final demonstration of his genius as a musician, looking forward, like Beethoven's last quartets, to new vistas in musical technique, in the character of Kundry we find brought to its finest flower his long study of drama and human character, and ability to blend innumerable sources into a theatrical and cohesive whole.*

The sources of *Parsifal* are similarly complex and again blended with dramatic coherence in Wagner's libretto. It is an individual achievement and the product of a lifetime's study of varied religions and religious myths, synchronised at last with Wagner's own instinctive faith in the ultimate strength of spiritual love as symbolised by Christ. This was heightened in his later years by contact with Cosima's deep Roman Catholic beliefs (inherited from her father, Liszt) and his own interest in Buddhism, vegetarianism and anti-vivisection propaganda. The profound compassion associated with the death of the swan in Act I – its slaying epitomised as a sin against God – cannot fully be understood without knowledge of these last two strands in Wagner's later life: strands, of course, with the social allegories of *The Ring*, which linked him so strongly, in spite of many differences, with his disciple Bernard Shaw.

The Prelude of *Parsifal*, like that of *Lohengrin*, is a sustained development of the atmospheric theme of the Holy Grail. Its opening *motif*, symbolising the Eucharist, is based on a plainsong melody similar to a Gregorian chant: in various forms, motivating Amfortas' pain and the Holy Spear, it is to permeate the score:

Its simple purity, unaccompanied in effect, is elaborated later with soft *arpeggios* and a rippling over-current on the strings, and

* For a fuller study of Kundry, from which some of the above derives, readers are referred to my article, "Wagner and Kundry", published in *The Music Review* (Vol. 13, No. 1) of February, 1952 (Ed. Geoffrey Sharp: pub. W. Heffer of Cambridge).

165

when it returns in simple form again it is in minor key, strangely poignant in effect. The second theme, associated with the Grail or its temple Montsalvat, is also to play a significant mystical part in the score:

It is, in fact, based on the Dresden "Amen" still sung at the Court Chapel in Wagner's time. Still in the key of A flat, much favoured by Wagner, we find, too, the *motif* of Faith, a splendid and expansive melody which, transformed, is to be heard often in the music of Gurnemanz, the faithful knight of Titurel, one-time chief guardian of the Grail:

With the *motif* of the Spear or Lance, which is actually the final fragment of the Eucharist melody which opens the opera, these themes are to play a dominant part in the musical fabric, especially in the Grail scenes and scenes of direct religious application.

The continuity of the Prelude is hardly broken by the rise of the curtain, to disclose a forest scene in the domain of the Grail, with a rising path towards the castle of Montsalvat and a deep-set lake just out of sight. Gurnemanz and two youthful Esquires are asleep under the trees, but he wakes them with the coming of the dawn, and at the sounding of the Grail theme on trumpets from the castle. Amfortas, the 'fisher-king' who is also Titurel's son and present guardian of the Grail, will be coming to bathe his wound in the lake; but of the cause of his suffering we do not yet hear. Two knights herald his coming, but are immediately interrupted by wild agitated music depicting the arrival of Kundry on her horse:

A savage creature with tangled black hair, dark piercing eyes and snakeskin girdle, she brings a crystal phial containing an Arabian balm for Amfortas' wound, and her offering of it is character-istically abrupt:

Her taciturnity, inherent in Wagner's drawing of her in drama and music (for by now the two were with him inseparable), leaps from the brief phrase, and the abrupt change of key emphasises her truculence. She rejects thanks later with equal brusqueness ("*Ich helfe nie*"), though how much of this fear of thanks and longing for unpaid service is rooted in guilt we are yet to learn. She now flings herself on the ground and is forgotten with the coming of Amfortas, whose note of unassuaged suffering is pierced by his recitation of the Promise:

the prophecy of the guileless Fool (*der reine Tor*) who, moved by pity, shall prove both his healer and Saviour of the Grail. He thanks Kundry, who rejects his thanks harshly as we have seen, and when the procession has passed Gurnemanz tells the full story to the knights. It is an old-fashioned Wagnerian and theatrical device of imparting knowledge to the audience, and in some hands Gurnemanz' bass eloquence can be tedious; but the story is a vital and mysterious one, and a great singer and artist like Ludwig Weber in our time can transform the character with a gentle spirituality that gives a deep tenderness and strength to the drama, and illuminates what Wagner, the artist, must have had in mind.

His narration embraces the history, as far as it is known, of both Kundry and Amfortas. Kundry, the strange intruder, who was woken from a trance in the bushes by Titurel, serves the Knights of the Grail in expiation, perhaps, of some unknown sin in a former life. Her disappearances are as mysterious as her original appearance; and always when they occur some disaster befalls Montsalvat. She is a creature apart, her origins unknown; and it was during one of her long absences that the last catastrophe occurred. For Amfortas strayed from Montsalvat into the domain of Klingsor, the wizard who has vowed to destroy or dominate the Grail, and there Gurnemanz found him in the embrace of one of Klingsor's enchantresses: helpless with the Holy Spear* at his side. For Gurnemanz alone was the terrible sight of Klingsor seizing the spear and launching it into Amfortas' side, inflicting a wound which can only be healed by the same spear, as the Grail brotherhood can only be revived by the return of it. For Titurel, into whose keeping the Holy Vessel was given by angels, is now an old, ailing man, kept alive only by sight of the Grail in the Communion rite, and Amfortas, his titular successor, is too oppressed by his wound and sense of guilt to command the ritual.

Klingsor has triumphed like Lucifer, Son of the Morning: for like him he is a renegade, a Knight of the Grail expelled for his sins from Montsalvat. At the end of this great narration, interrupted spasmodically by the knights and abruptly savage Kundry, and in which Klingsor's dark, wild *motif* is first heard among the shining tokens of the Grail, Gurnemanz refers to the prophecy of the blameless Fool; and as he does so a wounded swan flies overhead and amid great disturbance falls lifeless to the ground.

All animals are sacred in the land of the Grail, and when the shy, uncouth youth Parsifal is discovered with bow and arrows, he is aroused to pity and remorse by Gurnemanz' remonstrance. When in sudden grief he breaks his bow and flings it to the ground, Gurnemanz wonders if perhaps this guileless boy, who seems not to know his own name, may be the redeemer they await. Kundry tells more of him. As Gurnemanz guessed he is nobly born, the son of Gamuret who was slain in battle before his birth. Therefore his mother, Herzeleide (Heart-in-Sorrow), has reared him in the forest without knowledge of knighthood or arms; but the boy, nevertheless, has been lured away by the sight of a glittering band of knights, and while he has roamed the forest his mother, Kundry harshly relates, has died of grief.

Parsifal, uncorrupted by knowledge of good or evil and therefore quite thoughtless in his actions, is shattered by this news and attacks Kundry; but Kundry, says Gurnemanz, never lies, and when at this the boy trembles and feels faint, it is she who fetches water from the spring and hands him the horn from which to drink. "I never do good" is her fierce characteristic reply to Gurnemanz' praise, and there follows a short passage of the utmost dramatic significance. A heaviness seems to weigh on her, and

* It was Wagner's own inspiration to make this spear of the legend the lance with which Longinus pierced the side of Christ on the cross.

168

Kirsten Flagstad as Kundry, Covent Garden, 1951

with faltering steps she approaches a thicket, yearning for rest and sleep. But the very word "*Schlafen!*" awakes a dread in her, and for a moment she resists, but vainly, the oblivion falling on her. Then she stumbles into the wood, fatalistically resigned, and is seen no more.

The sun is now high, and the procession returning. Gurnemanz resolves to let Parsifal watch the holy service of the Grail, and as he leads the wondering youth to Montsalvat the forest vanishes and is replaced by a great gateway and finally the Hall of the Grail, where he places Parsifal in the shadows and bids him note all that passes. The music accompanying this journey has an impressive grandeur, in which the strongly accented *motif* of the Montsalvat Bells rings out in a rhythmic splendour:

A procession of knights enters for the service of the Eucharist, with Amfortas on a bier and the veiled shrine containing the Holy Grail. As the knights arrange themselves around the tables, a three-part chorus of youths' voices is heard from high in the dome, and another in four parts of children higher still, intoning the *motif* of Faith. These layers of chorus – knights below, youths

and children above – has a beautiful and original effect.

The voice of old Titurel is now heard (he is never seen) calling on his son from the crypt to reveal the Grail; Amfortas resists, and his re-awakened agony is expressed in many *motifs*. But he is finally overcome and the Grail uncovered. As the lights dim, the deeper strings vibrate in the orchestra, the children's choir floats mysteriously from the distance, and finally a ray of light descends from the darkness, lighting the Grail in a deep crimson. Amfortas waves the chalice solemnly to and

'Götterdämmerung' Act II: "Schlafst du, Hagen, mein Sohn?" Dezsö Ernster as Hagen, Otakar Kraus as Alberich, Covent Garden 1954

fro, and when he sets it down the glow of the Grail fades, and light returns to the Hall.

The Holy Communion, the celebration of the Last.Supper, now takes place, and the thanksgiving of the chorus is permeated by the theme of the Grail. The suffering Amfortas is carried away, and the procession of knights and youths follows, to the chime of the Bells. Parsifal and Gurnemanz are alone: but the boy is uncomprehending and apparently unmoved by compassion, and the disappointed Gurnemanz thrusts him out of the castle, exasperated by his stupidity. Yet as Gurnemanz, too, departs, we hear the voice of an alto repeating the Promise, while the choir in the dome replies softly with the themes of the Grail and the Spear. And we know, as Gurnemanz does not, that Parsifal is the promised 'blameless Fool', not ready yet for his burden.

The second act brings us into the contrasting domain of Klingsor, whose evil magic has brought forth a flower garden in the desert, with his castle in the midst. The flower garden and its maidens are a trap for wandering knights, many of whom remain ensnared; but we first meet Klingsor in his tower, with its vessels of necromacy and witchcraft, and the darkly tempestuous orchestral prelude, in sombre B minor key, is based almost entirely on the Klingsor *motif*:

Klingsor is conjuring Kundry, "Rose of Hades", to his service: she is the chief of his seductresses, and only he can resist her charms and therefore wield absolute power over her. In one of the mediaeval legends Klingsor was castrated by the father of a princess he had seduced. By a terrifyingly keen psychological stroke, Wagner makes him self-castrated, in an attempt to overcome the lust that lost him the Knighthood of the Grail. But the evil of his nature, fermented by resentment, has merely flowed into other channels. His Eunuchhood has given him a source of power which he is quick to grasp can be used for purposes of vengeance, and to gain ultimate control of Montsalvat. But like many who find an outlet for their personality in evil, he is unhappy and frustrated, as the lash of Kundry's scorn at his condition quickly reveals. He is aware, like Milton's Satan, of a Paradise Lost, and so touches tragedy, although the shape of the plot did not allow Wagner to develop the character as he might have done.

171

'Parsifal', Act I, Bayreuth production by Wieland Wagner.

Kundry rises in the bluish light of his incense like one asleep, and her resistant shrieks, as characteristic as the wild laughter which at other times heralds her approach, give her something of the terror and anguish we associate with Greek drama. We learn now that her service to the Grail is an atonement, and although Klingsor beats down her agonised reluctance it is in some ways only half a victory. As is obvious in the scene later with Parsifal, the passion and remorse, the longing for redemption, are cleavages in Kundry's own nature. In her duality lies her curse and the fascination of her powerful personality.

Parsifal is Klingsor's immediate concern, for he realises that he, the 'innocent Fool' of the prophecy, is potentially master of the Grail and his own strongest enemy. It is he Kundry must seduce and render helpless. Appalled and attracted, she can only give way before the double power of Klingsor and her own nature. In his magic mirror Klingsor now sees Parsifal, who has wandered from Montsalvat across the desert, on the battlements, lustily fighting the renegade knights of the garden. And as he watches the tower sinks from view and we are in Klingsor's luxurious garden.

Parsifal stands innocent and amazed on the battlements, and

among the exotic flowers a bevy of maidens discuss in tumultuous chorus the sights they have seen as their beloved knights fall to the boy's sword. But their ardour has no basis of love: their mourning quickly melts before the fascinating aspect of their new playmate. Their song takes on a seductive sweetness as they gracefully weave about the boy, innocently charmed by these flowers come to life. The vocal part-writing is elaborate, divided among two groups of singers and two full choruses (each group and chorus divided into three); but the melodies intertwine with an aerial lightness:

But soon they begin to quarrel as to ownership of the boy, and his interest turns to impatience. It is held again, by a new note: for as the maidens scatter Kundry's voice is heard, silvery and enticing, for the first time in the opera sounding Parsifal's name:

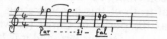

It echoes the Promise *motif* and ensnares Parsifal like a fine-spun silken thread; and as he turns, Kundry herself, unrecognisably transformed into an Eastern beauty, is seen reclining on a bed of flowers.

In the remarkable scene that follows, Kundry shows herself no ordinary seductress but a psychologist of some shrewdness. A lullaby-like figure in the orchestra has accompanied her tranquil dismissal of the maidens (no serious rivals, they, as they well know) and it is to Parsifal's feelings for his mother that she first appeals, in the gentle 'Herzeleide' Narration in which she relates how she watched his childhood from a baby at his mother's breast:

She tells, too, of Herzeleide's grief at Parsifal's disappearance, and her death: not harshly, now, as in the first act, but meltingly, so that Parsifal in his remorse seems ready to fall into her deceptively maternal arms. Promising him comfort in distress, she imprints on his lips a lingering kiss: and that very kiss is her undoing, bringing the wisdom she had promised Parsifal too soon. He springs up from the snare with his hand to his side, and in the pain of Amfortas' wound understands in a mystical flash that it was in Kundry's arms that the Grail knight was betrayed and received his wound, and that the torment of love possessing him will betray him too if he yields to it. In a trance he sees the Holy Grail (its *motif* swells in the background), and at last understands its significance. The cry in his heart is Christ's cry for a Redeemer to remove the pollution, and this at Montsalvat he had failed to hear. His own cry, now, is a cry of guilt.

It is a strange and illuminating passage, which captured the imagination of Shaw as an instance of Wagner's genius: "...that long kiss of Kundry's from which he (Parsifal) learns so much is one of those pregnant simplicities which stare the world in the face for centuries, and yet are never pointed out except by great men." The effect on Kundry is electrifying: her reaction is not the expected one of the woman scorned (that comes later, under the lash of Parsifal's contempt), but a still more passionate admiration. The psychological truth of this is penetrating. It is the purity in Parsifal, as it was the purity in Christ (of whom Parsifal is an allegorical parallel) that attracts her; and it is Kundry's curse that while her love can only be awakened by the spiritually pure or ascetic, that love remains bound, for all its spiritual yearning, to the demands of her passionate flesh. She recognises in Parsifal her Redeemer; yet by a subtle process of self-deception convinces herself that her redemption and Parsifal's will come after an hour of love in each other's arms.

In the throes of this spiritual conflict she tells for the first time the story of her mocking of the Saviour, and her endless wandering and bondage to evil until He returns to her, as He (Parsifal) now has. Kundry's music, often violent in its octave and two-octave intervals, its chromaticism as marked as Klingsor's, is strongly characteristic in this outburst, and it is probably not by accident that the part is composed for a voice of high dramatic soprano and low *mezzo* range: the tonal variety gives colour to the 'split' personality. Yet as we have seen her music can melt into tender-

174

ness; and there is a superb contrast here in the narration of her mocking of Christ, with its tremendous interval:

followed after a pause of two bars by the tender description of the look He then gave her, sorrowing and unforgettable:

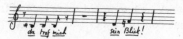

We remember Isolde's remembrance of Tristan's look, and how often the word '*blick*' occurs in revealing relationships in Wagner's works. His own eyes, people frequently noticed, were exceptionally large, brilliant and expressive, and doubtless equally capable of speaking glances, romantic and the opposite.

Her tormented laughter, her curse, find their place in this narration, but Parsifal is unmoved. Redemption for them both, he says quietly, lies in resisting temptation; and perhaps because she realises he speaks the truth her anger and resistance are inflamed. Now at last she commands Klingsor to stay him, at the same time calling on the desert to block Parsifal's way back to Montsalvat should he escape. Across the world he shall wander, but never find the path to end his quest. It is a curse we shall see partly fulfilled; but Klingsor's appearance with the Holy Spear cannot hold him now. The wizard launches it but it remains static above Parsifal's head. Parsifal grasps it, and making the sign of the cross with it destroys Klingsor's domain, which vanishes as into dust. Only the desert remains, strewn with withered flowers. And for Kundry, fallen with a shriek at his feet, Parsifal has only the significant words: "You know where to find me again". A grown man now, the spear in his hand, he strides into the arid wilderness, while she watches him in desolate despair.

The third act opens on the edge of the forest, where Gurnemanz has built a hut. The Prelude reveals his sorrowing thoughts, musing on so much of the past, and it depicts as well Parsifal's endless search. It is spring, the meadows carpeted with flowers; but Gurnemanz himself is now greatly aged, as we see when he emerges from the hut, dressed as a hermit. Groans from the nearby thicket have attracted him, and he recognises Kundry's cry. Hastening to the bushes he draws them apart and attempts to arouse her. How long has she lain there? Winter is past, it is now the spring. He rubs her stiffened limbs and she awakes from her trance with a cry. Although physically the Kundry of Act I, she is strangely changed: her hair is combed, her face, once so rough and tormented, placid, her manner calm and resigned. Perhaps, thinks Gurnemanz, the fact that it is Good Friday morning has wrought this change in her.

Silently she rises, and as she moves towards the hut to resume her interrupted work as handmaid there escape from her the two broken words that constitute her sole verbal contribution to the final act:

Fritz Wolff as Parsifal, Act III

The musical echo of her opening *"Nimm du! Balsam..."* is striking and characteristic. She fetches a pitcher from the hut and takes it to the spring; and by a sign indicates to Gurnemanz the approach of a stranger through the woods.

The orchestra warns us it is Parsifal, but the knight in black armour has his visor lowered, and Gurnemanz can only wonder. His spear drooping, with weary steps the stranger seeks a grassy mound, and sits. To Gurnemanz' questions he makes no reply, but on the old man's reference to the holy day he plants his spear in the earth, removes his helmet, and kneels in silent prayer. Gurnemanz at once recognises him as the youth of long ago, and the spear also; and the recognition is mutual. It is indeed the Grail Spear, says Parsifal, which he has never, even in direst stress during his wanderings, used in battle, remembering its holy nature. He is moved and saddened by Gurnemanz' news. Titurel is dead, Amfortas in his agony has refused the unveiling of the Grail, and Montsalvat has lost its power.

Parsifal's instinct is one of guilt: through his early blindness to his mission these tragedies have come to pass. A faintness assails him, and as in Act I it is Kundry who brings water and sprinkles his face with it. For Gurnemanz, now, there is no doubt: Parsifal is his new King, the prophesied Redeemer and guardian of the Grail. And as if to emphasise this, Kundry, Magdalene-like, bends and washes the knight's feet with holy water from a golden phial, and dries them with her long hair. Parsifal, in turn, baptises her, and as the meadows begin to sparkle in the sunlight there occurs the lovely passage of Good Friday music still played in concerts throughout the world, especially at Easter: mystic and serene, its roots in some visionary inspiration Wagner himself may only have dimly apprehended:

The oboe line develops into a symphonic texture, over which Gurnemanz' and Parsifal's voices break gently, like advancing and receding summer waves. In this tender glory of sound Parsifal kisses Kundry silently on the brow. *"Ich sah' sie welken die einst mir lachten: ob heut' sie nach Erlösung schmachten?"* ("I saw them wither who mocked me: do they now long for redemption?"): the identification with Christ is implicit in his words. Then, having been baptised by Gurnemanz himself, he is dressed by the old man in the robe of a Knight of the Grail, and makes his way with his two companions to Montsalvat. As the scene changes we once again hear the Bells in their solemn rhythm.

The great funeral march – the funeral march of Titurel – that follows has a spacious nobility almost as fine in its way as Siegfried's in *Götterdämmerung*. Trumpets and trombones sustain it above the throbbing of the Bells:

We are present, now, in the Hall of the Grail, where a procession bears Titurel's coffin across the stage. Another procession carries Amfortas and the veiled shrine, and while the choruses intone his guilt he himself breaks into an agony of remorse. Why unveil the Grail again, to revive a life he would far prefer to lose? In a delirium he begs the knights to kill him and end his misery. But as they stand appalled it is Parsifal who steps forward; only the spear that caused the wound, he says, may heal it. And as he stretches out his arm and touches the wound with the lance, Amfortas, supported by Gurnemanz, shows the miracle has occurred.

Parsifal now commands the Grail to be uncovered, and as he kneels in prayer before it a shaft of celestial light descends on it. To the wondering chorus of Grail *motifs* a white dove flutters from the dome and hovers over Parsifal's head. Amfortas and Gurnemanz kneel in homage before him, and as the new guardian of the Grail waves the chalice gently aloft, Kundry sinks, without even a cry, her eyes fixed tranquilly on Parsifal, to the ground in death and release.

It is a tribute to the power with which Wagner has conceived her that speechless, in shadow, she remains a potent figure in our consciousness, and moving to the last. Our last thoughts centre on her, no less than on Parsifal and Amfortas, the living redeemer and redeemed.

In the later passages of this work particularly we feel something altogether new in Wagner's music: the *motifs* are woven with technical ingenuity and magic as before, but the chromaticism when it occurs is not the chromaticism of *Tristan*, and the music strangely casts its light forward into the twentieth century. At the

178

RICHARD WAGNER

same time there is a sense of an inspiration not of this earth. This mystic masterpiece is as inevitably Wagner's last work as Shakespeare's *The Tempest* strikes us as being a more conscious philosophical synthesis and farewell to the stage. In the one the music, in the other the poetry, touches the cloud-capp'd towers of another world. Wagner himself knew *Parsifal* to be his swan-song; and although he had long cherished the idea of turning from opera to symphonic music, the span of life was too short for such dual achievements. His great symphonies remained revolutionary dreams; his great operas live today, a unique achievement which no musician has successfully followed, though his ideas on music-drama have been absorbed to the good of the stage.

Wagner's grandsons: Wieland (left) and Wolfgang Wagner

Bibliography

This short selected list of books for further reading is based on a few of the more important works and excludes many repetitive biographies and studies, as well as books dealing with individual Wagner operas or concerned with them only incidentally.

RICHARD WAGNER : *My Life* (English translation of Wagner's auto-biography to the year 1864, *Mein Leben*. In two volumes.)
Constable, London 1911; rev. ed. *Dodd, New York 1924.*

RICHARD WAGNER'S PROSE WORKS
(Trans. by William Ashton Ellis. In eight volumes). A complete and invaluable collection divided into volumes under the following headings:
Vol. 1 The Art Work of the Future.
Vol. 2 Opera and Drama.
Vol. 3 The Theatre.
Vol. 4 Art and Politics.
Vol. 5 Actors and Singers.
Vol. 6 Religion and Art.
Vol. 7 In Paris and Dresden.
Vol. 8 Posthumous, etc. including translations of *Siegfrieds Tod* and Wagner's sketches for *Das Liebesmahl der Apostel* and *Die Sieger.*
Kegan Paul, London 1892–1899.

THE LETTERS OF RICHARD WAGNER
(The Burrell Collection, edited with notes by John Burk).
Macmillan, New York 1950; Gollancz, London 1951.

LETTERS OF RICHARD WAGNER TO MATHILDE WESENDONCK
(Trans. by Ashton Ellis).
Grevel, London 1904; Scribner, New York 1907.

CORRESPONDENCE OF WAGNER AND LISZT
(Trans. by Dr. Hueffer. In two volumes).
Grevel, London 1888.

RICHARD WAGNER'S LETTERS TO AUGUST ROECKEL
(Trans. by Eleanor C. Sellar).
Arrowsmith, Bristol.

ERNEST NEWMAN : *Life of Richard Wagner* (In four volumes).
Cassell, London 1933–37; Knopf, New York 1933–41.

WILLIAM ASHTON ELLIS: *Life of Wagner* (Being an authorised English

version of C. F. Glasenapp's *Das Leben Richard Wagners*. Volumes V and VI (to 1859) were additions by Ashton Ellis. In six volumes).
Kegan Paul, London 1900–1908.

HOUSTON STEWART CHAMBERLAIN
: *Richard Wagner* (The author, a critic, married Wagner's and Cosima's daughter, Eva; trans. by G. A. Hight. In two volumes).
J. B. Lippencott, Philadelphia, 1897.

RICHARD DUMOULIN-ECKART
: *Cosima Wagner* (Trans. by C. Phillips. In two volumes).
Knopf, New York 1930.

PAUL BEKKER
: *Richard Wagner, His Life in His Work* (Trans. by M. M. Bozman).
Dent, London 1924 and 1931 Norton, New York 1931.

ALBERT LAVIGNAC
: *The Music Dramas of Richard Wagner* (One of the first and most extensive studies of music and text by the Professor of Harmony at the Paris Conservatoire, with illustrations and diagrams. Trans. by Esther Singleton).
Service and Paton, London 1888; Dodd, New York 1896 and 1905.

BERNARD SHAW
: *The Perfect Wagnerite: a Commentary on the Ring of the Nibelungs* (Included also in *Major Critical Essays*, Constable, London 1932 and 1948; the collections of Shaw's music criticism, *London Music*, 1888–89, – Constable, London 1937 and 1950 – and *Music in London*, 1890–94, – three volumes, Constable, London 1932 and 1956 – also contain much commentary on Wagner).
Grant Richards, London 1898; Brentano's, New York 1902.

ERNEST NEWMAN
: *Wagner Nights* (The American book is published under the title *The Wagner Operas*.)
Putnam, London 1949; Knopf, New York 1949.

LAWRENCE GILMAN
: *Wagner's Operas.*
Farrar and Rinehart, New York 1937.

CUTHBERT HADDEN
: *The Operas of Wagner* (Illustrated with 24 plates in colour from drawings by Byam Shaw.)
Nelson, London; Jack, London and Stokes, New York 1908.

AYLMER BUESST
: *The Nibelung's Ring.*
G. Bell, London 1932 – rev. ed. Newman Neame 1952.

JESSIE L. WESTON
: *The Legends of the Wagner Dramas.*
D. Nutt, London 1903.

WAKELING DRY
: *Nights at the Opera: Wagner* (Acknowledging help of Frau Cosima Wagner among others. Principally useful in giving cast-lists of original German and some first foreign productions and source material. *Die Meistersinger* omitted.)
Hodder and Stoughton, London.

'Tristan und Isolde': Kirsten Flagstad as Isolde (Metropolitan debut, 1935)

A Selected Discography
from Great Britain and America

This list does not include historical recordings or standard-play (78) records, but only a selection of long-play records available at time of writing to the general public.

THE FLYING DUTCHMAN

Complete recordings

Hermann Uhde, Ludwig Weber, Astrid Varnay, Elisabeth Schartel.
Bayreuth Festival Orchestra and Chorus, conducted by Joseph Keilberth.

3-Decca LXT 5150-2 (G.B.)
3-London A-4325 (U.S.A.)

Dietrich Fischer-Dieskau, Gottlob Frick, Marianne Schech, Rudolf Schock.
Chorus and Orchestra of the German State Opera, Berlin, conducted by Franz Konwitschny

E.M.I. SLS-760, ASD.385-6-7
RLS-665, ALP.1806-7-8 (G.B.)
Angel S-3616C-L (U.S.A.)

Excepts

Overture
Berlin Philharmonic Orchestra, conducted by Rudolf Kempe.   HMV ALP1513 (G.B.)

Vienna Philharmonic Orchestra, conducted by Wilhelm Furtwängler.   Electrola 90023 (U.S.A.)

TANNHAUSER

Complete recording

Marianne Schech, August Seider, Otto von Rohr.
Munich State Opera Orchestra, conducted by Robert Heger.

4-Urania 211 (U.S.A.)

Excerpts

Overture; Venusberg Music; Elisabeth's Greeting;
'Freudig begrussen'; 'Gar viel und schon';
'Blick ich umher'; Elisabeth's Prayer;
'O du mein holder Abendstern'; 'Inbrunst im Herzen'
Leonie Rysanek, Wolfgang Windgassen,
Josef Greindl, with the Bavarian Radio Chorus,
the Wurtemberg State Orchestra,
conducted by Ferdinand Leitner.

> Deutsche Grammophon DGM
> 190-69 (G.B.)
> Decca 9928 (U.S.A.)

Overture and Venusberg Music
Women's Chorus of the Berlin
State Opera with the Berlin Philharmonic Orchestra,
conducted by Rudolf Kempe.

> HMV ALP1513 (G.B.)
> Angel 35574 (U.S.A.)

'Dich, teure Halle', Elisabeth's Prayer
Aase Nordmo-Lovberg recital
(also excerpts from Lohengrin and Die Walküre)

> Columbia 33CX1651 (G.B.)
> Angel S-35715 (U.S.A.)

LOHENGRIN

Complete recording

Wolfgang Windgassen, Eleanor Steber,
Hermann Uhde, Astrid Varnay, Josef Greindl.
Bayreuth Festival Chorus and Orchestra,
conducted by Josef Keilberth.   5-Decca LXT 2880-4 (G.B.)

Anneliese Kupper, Hans Braun, Lorenz Fehenberger,
Ferdinand Frantz, Otto von Rohr.
Bavarian Radio Orchestra and Chorus,
conducted by Eugen Jochum.   4-Decca DX-131 (U.S.A.)

Excerpts

'In fernem Land'; Lohengrin's Farewell
Wolfgang Windgassen recital
(also excerpts from Rienzi, Götterdämmerung,
Siegfried, Tristan und Isolde, Parsifal, Tannhauser)

> Deutsche Grammophon DGM 19106 (G.B.)

DAS RHEINGOLD

Complete recording

Kirsten Flagstad, George London, Gustav Neidlinger,
Set Svanholm, Eberhard Waechter, Paul Kuen,
Waldemar Kmentt, Walter Kreppel, Kurt Böhme,
Claire Watson, Jean Madeira.
Vienna Philharmonic Orchestra,
conducted by Georg Solti.

3-Decca LXT 5495-7 [SXL 2101-3] (G.B.)
3-London A-4340 [1309] (U.S.A.)

DIE WALKÜRE

Complete recording

Martha Mödl, Ludwig Suthaus, Leonie Rysanek,
Ferdinand Frantz, Gottlob Frick, Margarete Llose,
Vienna Philharmonic Orchestra,
conducted by Wilhelm Furtwängler.

5-HMV ALP1257-61 (G.B.)
5-Electrola 90100-4 (U.S.A.)

Excerpts

'*Ho-jo-to-ho*'; '*War es so schmahlich*'; '*Du zeugtest ein edles
Geschlecht*'; *Wotan*'s *Farewell*
Frida Leider and Friedrich Schorr,
with the Berlin State Orchestra,
conducted by Leo Blech
(also excerpts from *Die Götterdämmerung*)

HMV COL-105 (G.B.)
Angel 105 (U.S.A.)

'*Der Manner Sippe*'; '*Du bist der Lenz*'
Kirsten Flagstad recital
(also excerpts from Lohengrin and Parsifal)

Decca LXT 5249 (G.B.)

SIEGFRIED

Excerpts

Forest Murmurs
Cleveland Orchestra,
conducted by George Szell.   Fontana CFL 1012 (G.B.)
Epic LC-3321 (U.S.A.)

'*Die Meistersinger*': Hans Hotter as Hans Sachs

'Tristan und Isolde': Act II, Metropolitan Opera, New York, 1961. Birgit Nilsson as Isolde, Jerome Hines as King Marke, Ramon Vinay as Tristan

Franz Lechleitner
with the Vienna Philharmonic Orchestra,
conducted by Hans Knappertsbusch.   Decca LXT2644 (G.B.)

'*Nothung, Nothung*'
Wolfgang Windgassen
with the Bamberg Symphony Orchestra,
conducted by Ferdinand Leitner.
(Also *Siegfrieds Tod* and excerpts from
Rienzi, Götterdämmerung, Lohengrin, Tristan and *Parsifal*.),
with the Munich Philharmonic Orchestra,
conducted by Arthur Rother.

Deutsche Grammophon
DGM19106 (G.B.)
Deutsche Grammophon 17059
(U.S.A.)

'*Heil dir, Sonne*'; *Love Duet*
Kirsten Flagstad and Set Svanholm
with the Philharmonia Orchestra,
conducted by Georges Sebastian.   HMV BLP 1035 (G.B.)
Electrola 60545 (U.S.A.)

GOTTERDAMMERUNG

Complete recording

.Kirsten Flagstad, Set Svanholm,
Egil Nordsjø, Waldermar Johnsen,
Per Grönneberg, Eva Gustavson.
Oslo Philharmonic Orchestra and
Norwegian Radio Orchestra and Chorus,
conducted by Oivin Fjedlstad.

6-Decca LXT5205-10 (G.B.)
6-London A-4603 (U.S.A.)

Excerpts

Prelude; Siegfried's Journey to the Rhine; Funeral March;
Brunnhilde's Immolation
Kirsten Flagstad
with the Vienna Philharmonic Orchestra,
conducted by Wilhelm Furtwängler.   HMV ALP1016 (G.B.)

Siegfried's Death
Lauritz Melchior
with the London Symphony Orchestra,
conducted by Robert Heger.
(also excerpts from *Die Walküre*)   Angel 105 (U.S.A.)

TRISTAN UND ISOLDE

Complete recordings

Kirsten Flagstad, Blanche Thebom,
Ludwig Suthaus, Josef Greindl,
Dietrich Fischer-Dieskau.
Philharmonia Orchestra and Covent Garden Chorus,
conducted by Wilhelm Furtwängler.

6-HMV ALP1030-35 (G.B.)
5-Angel 3588E (U.S.A.)

Birgit Nilsson, Fritz Uhl, Regina Resnik,
Tom Krause. Vienna Friends of Music Chorus
and Vienna Philharmonic Orchestra,
conducted by George Solti.

Decca SET.204-8 MET.204-8 (G.B.)
London A-4506 (Stereo: OSA-1502)
(U.S.A.)

Excerpts

Prelude, Act I; Liebestod
Vienna Philharmonic Orchestra,
conducted by Rudolf Kempe.

HMV ALP1638 (G.B.)

'*Doch nun von Tristan*'; *Liebestod*
Birgit Nilsson and Grace Hoffman
with the Vienna Philharmonic Orchestra,
conducted by Hans Knappertsbusch.

Columbia 33CX1522 (G.B.)
London 5537 [OS-25138] (U.S.A.)

Prelude, Act III
Detroit Symphony Orchestra,
conducted by Paul Paray.

Mercury 11056 (G.B.)
Mercury 50107 [90107] (U.S.A.)

DIE MEISTERSINGER

Complete recordings

Paul Schöffler, Gunther Treptow, Hilde Gueden,
Otto Edelmann, Anton Dermota,
Else Schurhoff, Karl Donch, Alfred Poell.
Vienna Philharmonic Orchestra and
Vienna State Opera Chorus,
conducted by Hans Knappertsbusch. 6-Decca LXT2659-64 (G.B.)
6-London A-4601 (U.S.A.)

Otto Edelmann, Friedrich Dalberg,
Erich Kunz, Heinrich Pfanzl,
Gerhard Unger, Elisabeth Schwarzkopf.
Bayreuth Festival Chorus and Orchestra,
conducted by Herbert von Karajan.

5-Columbia 33CX1021-5 (G.B.)

Ferdinand Frantz, Gottlieb Frick,
Benno Kusche, Gustav Neidlinger,
Gerhard Unger, Elisabeth Grummer,
Berlin Opera and Municipal Opera Chorus,
the Berlin Philharmonic Orchestra,
conducted by Rudolf Kempe.   5-HMV ALP1506-10 (G.B.)

Excerpts

Knappertsbusch recording from the complete opera;
cast given on page 190.
*Prelude; 'Am stillen Herd'; 'Fanget an'; 'Was duftet doch der Flieder';
'Wahn! Wahn! Uberall Wahn!'; Die selige Morgentraum-Deutweise';
'Aha! Da streicht die Lene'; 'Selig wie die Sonne'; Prize Song.
'Verachtest mir die Meister nicht'.*   Decca LXT5544 (G.B.)

*'Am stillen Herd'; 'Nun Meister, wenn's gefallt';
'Was euch zum Leide'; 'Fanget an'; 'Was duftet doch der Flieder';
'Wahn! Wahn! Uberall Wahn!'; 'Selig wie die Sonne';
'Silentium - Wach' auf'; Prize Song;
'Verachtest mir die Meister nicht'*
Wolfgang Windgassen, Annaliese Kupper, Herta Töpper
and Richard Holm
with the Wurtemberg State Orchestra,
conducted by Ferdinand Leitner.   Deutsche Grammophon
DGM19047 (G.B.)

Overture, Prelude, Act III
NBC Symphony Orchestra,
conducted by Arturo Toscanini.   RCA RB16136 (G.B.)

Bavarian Radio Symphony Orchestra,
conducted by Eugen Jochum.   Epic LC-3485 (U.S.A.)

PARSIFAL

Complete recording

Wolfgang Windgassen, Martha Mödl, Ludwig Weber,
George London, Hermann Uhde, Arnold van Mill.
Bayreuth Festival Orchestra and Chorus,
conducted by Hans Knappertsbusch.
(1951 Festival performance)

6-Decca LXT2651-6 (G.B.)
6-London A-4602 (U.S.A.)

Excerpts

> *Good Friday Music*
> NBC Symphony Orchestra,
> conducted by Arturo Toscanini.   RCA RB16135 (G.B.)

> Otto Edelmann
> with the Philharmonia Orchestra,
> conducted by Otto Ackermann.   Angel 35571 (U.S.A.)

> *Transformation Scene*
> Houston Symphony Orchestra,
> conducted by Leopold Stokowski.   Everest 6031 3031 (U.S.A.)

> *'Nein Parsifal'* - *'Ich sah das Kind'*
> Kirsten Flagstad recital
> (also excerpts from Lohengrin and Die Walküre)
>
> Decca LXT5249 (G.B.)

A note on the illustrations

The illustrations appearing in this volume were collected by the author from the following sources or loaned by herself:

Covent Garden Opera House: 58, 73, 87, 93, 121, 142, 145, 162, 169, 176.
Desmond Shawe-Taylor: 102.
E.M.I. Ltd.: 84, 85, 99, 104, 128, 135, 146, 161.
Harold Rosenthal: 69, 70.
Radio Times Hulton Picture Library: 2, 6, 9, 12, 15, 17, 19, 20, 22, 23, 24
25, 26, 27, 28, 29, 30, 40, 44, 46, 47, 54, 92, 97, 118–9, 137b, 152, 179.
Times Picture Library: 65, 120, 127, 155, 158, 172.

Acknowledgment is due to the following photographers or organisations:
Angus McBean: 162, 169.
Atwell, Chicago: 44.
Baron: 185
Bayreuth Festival: 65, 70, 74, 110, 112, 120, 127, 143, 155, 158, 164, 176.
Daguerre, Chicago: 85.
Denis de Marney: 145.
Derek Allen: 125, 128.
Fritz Schwennicke: 110, 120, 127.
Houston Rogers: 87, 93.
Keystone: 180.
Lauterwasser: 65, 158.
Nadar, Paris: 102.
Roger Wood: 70, 111.
Sabine Toepffer, Munich: 69.
Setzer, Vienna: 84.
Wickman, Oslo: 56.
Wilfrid Newton: 74, 121, 170.

1972-3-13
Q-T